THANK GOD FOR MERCY365

THANK GOD FOR MERCY365

Raymond F. Faircloth Sr., D. Min

ISBN: 979-8-89590-756-6 (Paperback)
Library of Congress Control Number 2026906447

Published 2026 by MERCY365 PUBLICATIONS in the United States of America

For information about special discounts or bulk orders, contact the author at *Raymondfaircloth@aol.com*

CONTENTS

FOREWORD by Raymond Faircloth, Jr. 1

FOREWORD by Melissa Faircloth Locklear 5

DEDICATION 7

APPRECIATION 9

PART ONE: GOD'S MERCY UPON MY LIFE

INTRODUCTION MERCY365 15

Song: MERCY365 23

CHAPTER ONE: This Is My Story, This Is My Song 27

Song: This Is My Story. This Is My Song. 35

CHAPTER TWO: The Free Will Holiness Church 37

CHAPTER THREE: My First Music Teacher 45

Song: The Vessel Called Victory 59

CHAPTER FOUR: My Calling into the Ministry 61

CHAPTER FIVE: My Best Friend Jenny 69

Song: Together Forever 75

CHAPTER SIX: Down to Night and Nothing 77

CHAPTER SEVEN: Dancing In the Rain 83

Song: At Last, At Last. My Past Is Past 91

CHAPTER EIGHT: This is Your Mission Field 93

Song: Your Mission Field 101

PART TWO: GOD'S MERCY UPON OTHERS

CHAPTER NINE: "I Came Here to Get Saved!" 107

CHAPTER TEN: Meet My Friend, Vince Moore..........................115

Song: My Blessing is on the Way 127

CHAPTER ELEVEN: The Runaway Preacher............................ 129

Song: The Lord Had Mercy On Me 137

CHAPTER TWELVE: Spiritual Transmission Failure 139

Song: God's Not Finished With You Yet................................. 147

CHAPTER THIRTEEN: "That Was Me One Day" 149

Song: That Was Me One Day 153

PART THREE: GOD'S MERCY FOR HEALING

CHAPTER FOURTEEN: Divine Healing.................................... 159

CHAPTER FIFTEEN: Healed By the Power of God 165

Song: I'm Healed (By the Power of God)................................ 173

CHAPTER SIXTEEN: Healing's Happening 175

Song: Healing's Happening... 181

PART FOUR: GOD'S MERCY BRINGS CELEBRATION AND PRAISES

CHAPTER SEVENTEEN: The Lord Is Worthy of My Praise 187

Song: The Lord Is Worthy of My Praise 195

CHAPTER EIGHTEEN: Glory to God in the Highest 199

Song: Glory to God in the Highest... 207

PART FIVE: MERCY AT SUNSET

CHAPTER NINETEEN: Home At Last 213

Song: "HOME" AT LAST 221

CHAPTER TWENTY: When We Meet Again 223

Song: When We Meet Again 231

CHAPTER TWENTY-ONE: There is a City 233

Song: There Is A City 243

THE SUMMATION OF MERCY365

CHAPTER TWENTY-TWO: Mercy Is More Than A Scripture ... 251

Song: Mercy Is More Than A Scripture 259

CONCLUSION 261

ABOUT THE AUTHOR 263

FOREWORD

by Raymond Faircloth, Jr.

Throughout my entire life, I've watched my father lead by example. The sermons he has preached and the songs he has written over the years have inspired countless people. But I'm not sure any of them were inspired more than I was. As a child, I would watch my dad play the piano and sing, then stand to preach and declare God's Holy Word. I wasn't just watching, I was learning while he was leading.

My dad encouraged me to sing the Gospel, and not just to sing, but to do it boldly…with an anointing from our Heavenly Father.

He didn't just take me to church; he allowed me, Ray Jr., along with my sister Melissa and my mom Jenny, to be part of the services he led.

Many times, we would join him on stage to sing a song we had rehearsed, and sometimes one we hadn't! But those moments planted a deep love for music in my heart. I wanted to play and sing just like my dad.

As I grew older, the roles shifted. I became the one playing while my dad sang the songs he had written…or whatever song the Lord laid on his heart. For him to allow me to serve as the worship leader in his church fulfilled lifelong dreams for me. It has truly been the honor of a lifetime.

Mom and Dad say that when I came home from the hospital, they dressed me in an outfit that said, "Daddy's Little Helper." Looking back, I'm honored that for most of my life I have stood beside my dad in ministry, helping however I could… but in reality, he was the one helping me.

I've watched the Spirit of God minister through the gift of songwriting that my dad carries. I started to list some of the songs that have impacted me in this short foreword, but honestly, there are too many to name. What I can say is that I know the stories behind most of them. I lived in the house where many of those stories came to life through song. I watched the Holy Spirit move on the hand of the author who penned them.

Songs that he has written have come from physical healing, the home-going of loved ones, Praise that was overflowing, Testimonies from others, and even short exhortations in Prayer services. The truth is, God has used my dad to write songs with incredible meaning.

I've had the honor of singing and playing most of his songs, and I love them all… But I will say… I think a highlight for me was sharing a couple of these songs while leading Camp Meeting Music in Falcon, NC, and witnessing the Holy Spirit fall all over the auditorium as we sang "The Lord is Great & Worthy of My Praise." It is my honor to recommend this long-awaited book, which contains the stories behind many of his songs.

To my dad… I love you, and I am proud of you. I am proud to be your son, and I am so thankful that you pointed me to Jesus. It is the joy of my life to serve the Lord with you.

Rev. Raymond Faircloth, Jr.

FOREWORD

by Melissa Faircloth Locklear

With the turn of every page, I found my heart gleaming with pride and joy. Many call this author “Ray”, “Pastor”, “Brother”, “Doctor”, “Reverend”, and “Friend”, but I have the greatest honor, I get to call him “DADDY”. I have been with him on this journey since 1980. That’s 45 years if you are counting. I have watched my dad lead with integrity. He always practiced what he preached.

This book is more than just a bunch of pages. It is his life, (our) life. The different seasons of ministry can be wonderful, but they can also be hard. There are good days, bad days, and great days. In all those seasons of life, it seemed like God would pour a song down deep in dad’s heart.

God would give him each song to help us, but it always amazed me how it ended up blessing so many more. I feel sure you, too, will be blessed.

All the songs have been written under the anointing of God. I have had the great privilege of singing many of them. “Home At Last,” “My Blessing Is On The Way,” “This Is Your Mission Field,” “Healed by the Power of God,” and the list goes on and on.

Just recently, I have found myself singing "Healing's Happening" over and over again. I feel confident I'm not the only one through the years who's found themselves singing, humming, or tapping their toes to one of them. These songs inspire, uplift, and encourage so many just as the author has for 70 years.

God handpicked Raymond and Jenny Faircloth to be my parents, and I certainly am glad He did. They have both taught me the importance of seeing the glass half full, not half empty. Dad is known for saying, "Don't let what you can't do- hinder what you can do, and if you'll do what you can with what you've got, God will take what you've got and turn it into a miracle"! WOW, what a powerful life lesson!

As you read this book, page by page, I believe the same anointing that dad felt while penning the words, you, too, will feel. Dad's goal has also been to point others to the Cross. So, take your time, read every line, and hear the heart behind every song.

Dad, I am proud of you! Thank you for teaching me about Jesus and for leading me to the cross. I pray that this book will bless many.

Melissa Ann Faircloth Locklear

DEDICATION

I dedicate this book, these stories, and these events to my beloved wife, Jenny, and to my children—Ray Jr. and his wife, Pam, and my daughter, Melissa, and her husband, Sammy.

I also lovingly dedicate it to my six incredible grandchildren—**Savannah, Carter, TaRanda, Alyssa, Aydan, Taylor,** and then there is the great-grand, **Colsen Smith.** Each child is truly a divine "**Great**" joy in my earthly life.

With heartfelt remembrance, I also give the deepest honor to my **Mom and Dad**, Clyde and Minnie Faircloth, and to my four brothers, Clyde, William, Charles, and Jerry, who have all entered into eternity. Each of them contributed and helped shape the foundation of my life in their own unique way. Their influence continues to guide me today.

APPRECIATION

As I reach 50-plus years in the preaching ministry, I think it's appropriate to thank those I consider "Giants of the Faith" who have personally encouraged me along the way. Some continue to shine as lights of inspiration for us who remain, while others have finished their race and reached the glorious City of God.

With deep heartfelt gratitude, I say Thank You to Bishop Ronald Mizell, Bishop Ronald Carpenter Sr, Bishop James D. Leggett, Bishop Elwood Long, Bishop Jimmy Whitfield, Bishop D. Chris Thompson, Bishop Danny Nelson, Bishop Doug Bartlett, Bishop T. Ryan Jackson, Bishop B.E. Underwood, Bishop A.D. Beacham Jr, Bishop Oris Hubbard and Rev. Lonnie Carter, along with so many Brothers and Sisters in ministry who have helped and encouraged me along the way.

A Very Special Thank You to a wonderful friend of my family, Rev. Angela Ivey, for her help and guidance throughout the completion of this project.

Deedy and Jean White, thank you for believing in the Christ that lives in me from the very first time we met in Shallotte, North Carolina. Thank you for being a prayer warrior for others.

A Message from Rev. Casey Fleet:

Over 13 years ago, God called me to preach under Ray Faircloth Sr. He had faith in me and trusted me before I even felt ready. Even before I was licensed, he gave me chances to serve, lead, and grow. Over the years, I've had the honor of serving under his guidance in various roles, and in every phase, he's been a constant source of wisdom, correction, and encouragement. The person I am in ministry today is a direct result of everything he invested in me. Through his leadership, I learned that ministry isn't just about big moments, but about consistency, faithfulness, and caring for people. His preaching and music have reminded me that *this* is our mission field (Chapter 8 of this book). I've seen what true leadership looks like. To my family and me, he will always be Pastor Ray.

A Message from Rev. Rich Burkett:

I first met Pastor Ray Faircloth, Sr., during the summer of 2014 when my family and I began attending what is now known as Mercy Church. This was also around the time that Pastor Ray began working at a prison and was influential in getting my wife a job there as well. It was through her working relationship with him that I began to get an understanding of who this man was outside the pulpit. And what I found is that he is consistent, genuine, and caring. He truly loves people. He embodies generosity. He symbolizes the Father's love for all people. I have been blessed to call him pastor, mentor, colleague, and most of all, friend.

MERCY AND GRACE WORK HAND IN HAND

Mercy is God **NOT** Giving Us what we actually deserve.
(Judgment, Condemnation, Etc.)

Grace is God Giving Us what we don't deserve.
(Agape Love, Forgiveness, Etc.)

Part One

God's Mercy Upon My Life

INTRODUCTION

MERCY365

Mercy is one of the words that we use often, preach passionately, and quote freely, yet it is far more demanding than many of us realize. Mercy is not proven by what we say; it is revealed by what we do. Scripture makes this clear. Jesus never allowed mercy to remain theoretical. He required it to be lived out, even when it was uncomfortable, costly, or inconvenient.

To understand this, we turn to two powerful teachings of Jesus, one from **Luke 10** and the other from **Matthew 18**. One exposes the emptiness of religious talk without compassion. The other warns of the terrifying consequences of receiving mercy without extending it. Together, they form a sobering picture of what mercy truly means.

As Jesus taught, "For unto whomsoever much is given, of him shall be much required" (Luke 12:48).

Mercy in Action: Luke 10:30–37

Jesus begins with a familiar story, one that still confronts us today—the parable of the Good Samaritan.

A man was traveling from Jerusalem to Jericho, a steep and dangerous descent. Somewhere along that road, he fell among thieves. They stripped him, beat him, and left him half dead. This man represents more than a single traveler; he reflects humanity itself—wounded by sin, broken by circumstances, and often left helpless by life's cruelty.

When Religion Walks Away

A priest came down that same road. He saw the man, but he passed by on the other side. Then a Levite arrived. He came closer. He looked. But he also walked away.

Both were religious men. Both knew the law. Both likely knew the Scriptures. Yet neither showed mercy.

Religion without compassion is empty. Seeing a need is not the same as meeting a need. Titles, positions, and knowledge cannot substitute for a heart moved by love.

Mercy from an Unexpected Source

Then came a Samaritan, an outsider, despised by Jewish society. Yet when he saw the wounded man, something happened within him: *he had compassion.*

Compassion is not passive. It moves toward pain, not away from it. The Samaritan went to the man. He touched his wounds. He poured in oil and wine. He lifted him onto his own animal. He took him to an inn. He stayed with him. And when he had to leave, he paid for his continued care and promised to return.

Mercy always costs something—time, comfort, resources, pride. But mercy is never wasted.

Jesus ended the story with a question that still echoes: "Which of these three proved to be a neighbor?"

The answer was simple: *"He who showed mercy."*

Then Jesus spoke words that allow no escape: **"Go and do likewise."**

Mercy is not optional. It is evidence of Christlike living.

The Horror of Mercy Withdrawn: Matthew 18:21–35

If Luke 10 teaches us what mercy looks like in action, Matthew 18 warns us what happens when mercy is withdrawn.

Peter approached Jesus with a sincere question: "Lord, how often shall my brother sin against me, and I forgive him? Up to seven times?"

In Peter's mind, seven times was generous.

Jesus responded, "Not seven times, but seventy times seven."

In the Kingdom of God, forgiveness is not counted— it flows from a transformed heart.

An Unpayable Debt

Jesus then told a parable of a servant who owed his king ten thousand talents—an unimaginable debt. It was impossible to repay. This servant represents us. Our sin debt before a holy God is far beyond our ability to settle.

When the servant begged for mercy, the king did something extraordinary: he forgave the entire debt.

This is incredible mercy. God does not merely delay judgment—He cancels the debt.

Mercy Withdrawn

Yet that same forgiven servant went out and found a fellow servant who owed him a hundred denarii—a small amount by comparison. Instead of mercy, he responded with violence. He ignored the plea that mirrored his own earlier cry. He had received forgiveness but refused to give it.

When mercy stops with us, we have misunderstood true mercy and grace reciprocation.

Heaven Takes Notice

Other servants witnessed this injustice and were grieved. They reported it to the king. Unforgiveness never exists in isolation. It affects families, churches, and the entire body of Christ.

The king summoned the servant and spoke chilling words: "You wicked servant… should you not also have had compassion?"

The forgiveness was revoked. The servant was delivered to torment.

Unforgiveness always leads to bondage—inner torment, spiritual unrest, and broken fellowship.

Jesus concluded with a warning that should cause every believer to pause: "So My heavenly Father also will do to you if each of you, from his heart, does not forgive his brother."

This is not about earning salvation. It is about living out a heart transformed by mercy and grace.

Mercy is not what we say; it is what we live.
It is not what we post, it is what we practice.
It is not what we claim, it is what we give.

As Micah declared, "What does the LORD require of you but to do justice, to love mercy, and to walk humbly with your God?" (Micah 6:8)

And Jesus promised, "Blessed are the merciful, for they shall receive mercy." (Matthew 5:7)

Mercy365 simply means Mercy every day, not just in a Scripture, but in our steps, our sacrifices, our forgiveness, and through our Agape love.

Remember, in the Kingdom of God…

Mercy received must become Mercy released.

THANK GOD FOR MERCY

MERCY365

A MERCY365 PRAYER

Dear God,

I pray for someone who may be reading this right now. I ask that You would allow them to feel the heart of this preacher when it comes to *Mercy365*, and when it comes to the mercy of God that is extended to the believer every single day.

Even in our flaws and our failures, our hang-ups and our mess-ups, your mercy still reaches us and restores us. Thank You, Lord.

I pray, if there be any lack that the reader may be feeling in their relationship with You, any emptiness, that it be satisfied with the understanding and clarity that **Jesus Christ is indeed the propitiation for our sins**, meaning, He covers the lack, when we come short.

Thank You for Your mercy that never fails.

In the Name of Jesus Christ,

Amen.

MERCY365

written, August 4, 2025

VERSE 1

The sun rolls up on another day.
Dusty roads and skies of gray.
A heart so heavy, a world so wide,
But Mercy walks with me,
Mercy……Three, Sixty-Five

CHORUS

Mercy in the morning, Mercy at night,
Through the shadows, through the light.
Every hour, every breath I'm alive,
He gives me Mercy, Mercy Three, Sixty-Five.

VERSE 2

The church bells ring, a little sparrow sings,
There's a hymn of hope for those bruised and broke.
Still Mercy's there, if you'll trust and climb,
Thank God for Mercy…, Mercy, Three, Sixty-Five.

CHORUS

Mercy in the morning, Mercy at night,
Through the shadows, through the light.
Every hour, every breath I'm alive,
He gives me Mercy, Mercy Three, Sixty-Five.

In Reflection

In childhood, mercy was always present in ways I didn't recognize as mercy. God's mercy included correction and protection that formed my character. While I never deserved it, God's steady love surrounded me, and continues to surround you and me today.

As I grew older, God called me to ministry, and with that came questions and choices. Marriage at a young age brought promises or covenants and responsibilities. I was learning how to stand on my own before I was 21, but I was never really on my own. God's Mercy was always there. It met me in my inexperience. It steadied me when I messed up. It softened sharp edges and redirected me when I wandered too far in my own confidence.

In this book, I share a handful of stories and original songs that show how God's mercy has impacted my life and the lives of others. I've seen His mercy extended in a mighty way, not just in salvation and restoration but also in healing and in the sunset of loved ones' lives. That's why I ultimately titled this *Thank God For Mercy365*. I need his renewed mercy daily in this robe of flesh, and I'm thankful that it's available not just to me, but to all who will believe and receive.

CHAPTER ONE

This Is My Story, This Is My Song

As I began writing and preparing for this book, I truly believed at the start the title would be *This Is My Story, This Is My Song*. Those words have echoed through my heart for years. They came from a lyric line in the beloved hymn **"Blessed Assurance,"** written by **Fanny Crosby**.

As I studied the origins of that hymn and reflected on its meaning, one truth became clear to me: everyone has a story, and if they are willing and will allow it, everyone can have a song. Scriptures call it A NEW SONG.

So, here it is. This is my story. This is my song…or at least a small collection of the stories and songs throughout my lifetime.

The Inspiration

Fanny Jane Crosby wrote thousands of Gospel songs and hymns during her lifetime. She passed away at the age of 95 on February 12, 1915. She was blind for her entire life except for her first six weeks. Yet it is evident that she was remarkably gifted. She never allowed her lack of physical sight to hinder her from expressing the vivid spiritual clarity of God's love, care, and promises for His children. In my opinion, no one has ever been more expressive of God's love toward His people than Fanny Crosby.

One day in 1873, Fanny was visiting with a friend, Mrs. Joseph Knapp, a musician and the wife of the founder of Metropolitan Life Insurance Company. During their visit, Mrs. Knapp played a tune on her piano, a melody she had recently composed. She then turned to Fanny and asked, "What does this tune say?"

After kneeling in prayer for a few moments, Fanny rose and decla*red,* "It says, 'Blessed assurance, Jesus is mine!'" Immediately, she began to dictate the verses to Mrs. Knapp, who wrote them down, fitting the words to the melody exactly as we sing it today.

The stories and songs throughout my life have included Rejection, Acceptance, Disappointments, Struggles, and many Victories.

Let me begin with what appeared to be a major setback at the time, only to find out later that God had a different plan, for which I am thankful.

Rejection Was Actually Redirection

I filled out an application with DuPont Corporation in 1975. I had just graduated from high school. I wasn't married yet. I wasn't pastoring. I was simply a young man trying to step into adulthood and find my way.

When the phone call came that they were interested in hiring me, it felt like the door had swung wide open. Clyde, Willie, and Charlie were already employed by DuPont and were making very good money. It appeared I was about to follow in their footsteps. I was going to be a new hire, I thought.

They sent me for a physical and hearing test. Everything checked out. Everything was on go. I was unofficially hired and scheduled to report for work on the next Monday morning.

It felt secure. It felt stable. It felt like the next logical step in life. But on Sunday, the day before I was to report, the phone rang again. This time it was a DuPont supervisor. He informed me that a hiring freeze had been implemented on Friday. Just like that… the job was no longer mine.

No Monday morning reporting.
No factory floor.
No DuPont career.

At the time, I was very disappointed, a closed door, a major setback as far as I was concerned.

But looking back now, I see it very differently.

Folks, that one phone call completely altered the direction of my life. Knowing that Willie and Charlie retired from DuPont, and knowing that I, too, could have possibly built a career there. I might have climbed a corporate ladder. I could possibly have invested decades in that path. And there's nothing wrong with

honest work like that. I submit that many fine people have faithfully provided for their families through that company.
But I can clearly see now, God had a different, and as far as I'm concerned, better assignment for me.

That hiring freeze was not an accident for Ray Faircloth.
It was not bad luck or poor timing on my part.
It was the providence of God.

Before I ever pastored a church…
God was already arranging my steps.

What looked like rejection was redirection.
What felt like loss was actually alignment.

And somewhere in heaven, I believe my grandmother's prayers were still rising before the Lord. She had prayed for me.
Prayed that I would serve God.
Prayed that I would answer His call.
She prayed that I would walk in His purpose.

That Sunday phone call was part of the answer.

Instead of clocking in at a plant on Monday morning, my life slowly but surely turned toward full-time ministry, toward preaching, toward singing, toward sharing my stories and my songs, toward becoming…… "The Singing Preacher."

I didn't see it clearly then. But mercy was already guiding me.
Mercy stepped in and said, "I have something else for you."
And I'm grateful.

Grateful for a closed door.
Grateful for that hiring freeze.
Grateful for the phone call that never allowed me to clock in.
Because that one interruption positioned me for a lifetime of ministry.

As I look back now, I can say with confidence:
It was part of His plan. It was part of my assignment.
And His Mercy was already at work in my life.

*****

That's just one of many stories that altered the direction of my life, from assignment to assignment, from pastorate to pastorate. Looking back, I can see how God moved me in seasons. Each transition felt uncertain at the time. Each change required trust. But every shift carried purpose.

"This is my story; this is my song…"

Those words are more than a lyric. They are a testimony.
And the stories and songs continue even to this day.

Although I ultimately chose a different title for this book, I felt strongly that this song and this testimony needed to be shared as part of *MERCY365*. It represents my journey. My redemption. My gratitude to God.

It is my way of giving praise for all He has done, for where He brought me from, for what He carried me through, and for where He will yet carry me.

MERCY365 is not just a theme. It is the thread that runs through every chapter of my life.

Every closed door.

Every open door.

Every unexpected turn.

Every answered prayer.

Folks, this is my story. This is my song.

And Mercy has been writing it all along.

THANK GOD FOR MERCY

MERCY365

THIS IS MY STORY, THIS IS MY SONG PRAYER

Dear God,

I ask that You grant blessings on the individual reading this page. Help them to understand that every day of our lives, our story is being written.

Not only did Fanny Crosby have a story, and not only does Ray Faircloth have a story, but this reader is living out their own story right now.

I pray Your blessings upon this individual as the story unfolds. May they walk high in Your divine will as well as Your purpose for their lives. Bless, in the city and bless, in the country. Everywhere they place their feet, allow favor and blessings of God upon their life.

As their story continues to unfold, may they experience Your guidance, Your provision, and Your mercy at every step.

I pray that their life will reflect Your goodness and that their story will bring glory to Your name.

This I pray in the Name of Jesus Christ.

Amen.

This Is My Story. This Is My Song.

Lyrics by Raymond Faircloth Sr. (October 10, 2025)

CHORUS

This is my story. This is my song.
I've been preaching this message for fifty years long.
Today I'm still preaching, with a passionate heart,
Because heaven is waiting. The banquet's about to start.

VERSE

This is my story. This is my song,
Heaven is waiting. It can't be too long.
The harvest is ready. Soon, God's Church will be gone.
Please hear what I'm saying. Hear the heart of this Song.

VERSE

They'll come from all nations, all kindred and tongue.
To join in that Banquet at life's setting sun.
I made my decision in the years of my youth.
I've been saved, I'm forgiven, and you can be, too!

CHORUS

This is my story. This is my song.
I've been preaching this message for fifty years long.
Today I'm still preaching, with a passionate heart,
Because heaven is waiting. The banquet's about to start.

CHAPTER TWO

The Free Will Holiness Church

The Roots of Mercy Run Deep

I often heard my mother say that she took me to the 4th Street Free Will Holiness Church when I was just two weeks old. Just one block up the street from the Holiness Church was the Wright Street Church of God, where my mom and Dad actually attended as children.

My Grandma Ruth Edwards Harker (Mom's Mother) and my Grandma Murleen Faircloth Lamb (Dad's Mother) were Sunday school teachers there.

One block in the opposite direction was the 4th and Marstellar Street Church of God, which later moved to Pine Valley and became the Pine Valley Church of God. I remember my Great Grandmother, Ella Watkins, who attended that Church.

So, on Sundays, Grandma Murleen would drop her off, then we'd go one block down and attend the Free Will Holiness church.

In my early childhood, Grandma Murleen would help me stand on a wooden box so the congregation could see and hear me singing over the wooden banister. That small church building was filled with praises of the saints and the sweet presence of the Lord. That was the soil where my faith and ministry first began to take root.

As a young boy, I would leave the Holiness Church after Sunday school to go to the little store on the corner (between the two churches) for a soda, then I'd go down to the Church of God for a few minutes, but I wouldn't go in. (I knew I had to get back to the Holiness Church before preaching started.) Here's why I went to the Church of God: I'd put my ear to the door at the entrance just to listen to the incredible anointed singing. I can't tell you what they sang, but I knew they felt every word. After listening for a few minutes, I'd make my way back to the Holiness Church where Grandma Murleen would give me a smile from the piano stool. It was her way of saying… thank you for being back on time.

It was in that same 4th Street Church that Jenny and I were united in holy matrimony on my 20th Birthday (April 3, 1976).
One day in the late 90s, Jenny and I rode by the old church, just to take a look and reminisce. As we drove towards the old building, I noticed the roof was starting to cave in.

It was clear to me, from the city's "condemned" notices on the doors and windows, that the old building where I had attended as a child would soon be demolished. Something stirred inside of me. I knew that once it was all removed, a tangible part of my childhood, the place of my spiritual beginning, would be gone.

A Mission Accomplished and a Precious Memento

So, I decided to do something kind of dangerous, which I probably shouldn't have, but I'm glad I did. I violated every posted warning and made my way inside that fragile, collapsing building. Roof fragments and ceiling tiles were hanging down; pieces of wood and debris were scattered across the floor. I kept hearing Jenny from the side door say, "Please be careful," as she could clearly see I had walked into a very dangerous situation.

But I was determined. I wanted a piece of the altar, just one little piece of the wood from that altar area where I had knelt as a young boy to ask Jesus to be my Savior. Living hours away, I was convinced that this would possibly be my only chance to retrieve any tangible reminder of the Church that I had been raised in. Once the church building was gone, the opportunity for a memento would be gone, too.

I walked and crawled in carefully, moving boards and whatever else was in my path. I made my way to the right side of the altar. the exact spot where I had knelt as a young boy to ask Jesus to be the Lord of my life so many years before.

There, among all the debris, I found a loose piece of wood from the altar. There it was, in my hand. A reminder of the place where Jenny and I stood exchanging vows years before. A keepsake of where my grandma lined up Jerry, Charlie, Willie, Clyde, and me, all just young boys, to be dedicated to the Lord.

That small piece of wood from the altar was like the big prize…. A reminder of where I watched my brothers kneel and pray, and the Easter and Christmas programs where we had stood doing our childhood parts. That small piece of altar was like the biggest fish to a fisherman, or the biggest deer to a hunter, to me. Though very small in size, it was incredibly huge in significance.

Today, that piece of board sits on or near my desk as a constant reminder of where and when I was saved. I've thought about it so many times, how the DNA from the tears of all the saints that have gone on had probably soaked into that little piece of wood after years of altar experiences, and how they could never be washed away.

I can assure you that that little piece of wood is one of the most valuable possessions that I have ever or will ever own.

Looking back, I think of our Pastors like Rev. B. G. Byrd, Johnny Pope, his brother Hovie, David Casey, George Jones, and George Fowler, who all left a lasting impression on my young heart. The Pope family especially impacted me. I can still see and hear them singing "The Heart That Was Broken for Me," and I remember Johnny and Hovie's father silently acting the song out like a mime.

The whole family worshiped with such sincerity. Back then, as a child, though I didn't truly understand what I was feeling, I knew, in my own way, that God was touching my heart.

Sitting on those old wooden pews, I watched and listened to Brother David and Sister Mary Casey sing:

That is why I'm thankful,
That's why I sing and shout.
God put something in my heart,
That I can shout about.

Those were indeed formative, impressionable moments, experiences that quietly began shaping my life in ministry.

As a young boy, Pastor David Casey invited me to ride with him to visit the sick and elderly. On one occasion, we visited a couple that I only remember as Brother and Sister Oxendine.

I remember Brother Oxendine asking Pastor Casey, "Did you bring a helper?"

Brother Casey smiled and said, “Yes, this is Little Ray. One day he’s going to be visiting the sick, praying for the sick, and preaching the gospel.”

******

The years have passed, and I am older now. Time has added lines to my face and stories to my heart. But I remain deeply thankful for the many messages of mercy I heard as a young boy, messages that would shape my life long before I understood their full meaning. Those sermons weren’t just words. They were seeds.

The roots of my raising run deep. When I look back on those childhood days, I can still feel the atmosphere of prayer. I can still hear the sounds of the saints calling my name before the Lord.

Before I knew about theology, I was learning about Mercy. Before I ever preached a sermon, God was already writing the sermon of my life through His Mercy and Grace.

It was in those early days, in simple church services, in heartfelt altar calls, in faithful preaching, that God began to call me. Though I didn’t fully understand it then. I was just a boy. But something deep inside me knew that my life belonged to God.
Looking back now, I see it clearly:

Mercy was shaping me, Mercy was protecting me and Mercy was preparing me.

And the roots of my raising still hold me steady today.

THANK GOD FOR MERCY

MERCY365

CHAPTER THREE

My First Music Teacher

My grandmother, Murleen Watkins Faircloth Lamb, known to everyone in my youth as *Sister Faircloth,* was my very first music teacher.

Long before I ever stood behind a pulpit, picked up a guitar, or sang in a church service, I learned about the importance of music by her side. Not necessarily music theory, but what she taught me went far beyond theory, melodies, and lyrics. Through her, I learned that music could be ministry, that a simple song could usher in the presence of God into a room, and that singing was another way to testify to or witness to God's goodness.

Some of the first songs I learned were simple gospel standards: "He's Got the Whole World in His Hands," "Gathering Flowers for the Master's Bouquet," and "Surely I Will, Lord." At the time, I didn't understand the depth of those words, but they took root in my heart. Years later, I would sing "Gathering Flowers for the Master's Bouquet" at more funerals than I can remember.

Even as a child, God was teaching me something important: that a song can bring comfort to the grieving, lift a heavy, broken heart, and remind hurting people of God's eternal hope. Long before I knew the language of ministry, I was learning the heart of ministry through music.

Some of my most treasured memories were made while visiting my Aunt Pearl (Mason) on Silver Lake Road. Those visits often turned into family worship services without anyone planning them. We would gather around the piano with songbooks in hand. Grandma would sit down at the keys, and before long, the room would be filled with music.

My cousin Tony would sing harmony, and my brother Charlie would often join in. It wasn't unusual for Jerry or Willie to be there also. You see, there was no performance, no spotlights, just family voices blending in harmony and sincerity.

We sang until our hearts were full. The songs weren't rushed, and no one was in a hurry to stop. Those moments were rich with faith, fellowship, and the unmistakable presence of God. Looking back now, I realize that those living room singings were shaping me as much as any church service ever could. Music wasn't something we *did*; it was something we *lived*. It was how we worshiped, how we connected, and how faith in God was being passed from one generation to the next.

Cottage Prayer Meetings

Music with Grandma didn't stop at family gatherings. On many occasions, I went with her to what were called cottage prayer meetings. These were small gatherings in homes, simple, humble, and powerful. Sometimes there was a piano, sometimes there wasn't. When there was no piano, I would bring my guitar. I didn't know a lot about the guitar then, just three chords: C, G, and D. But I also had a capo, and if you knew three chords and had a capo, you could play just about anything in the gospel songbook we used.

Those little meetings taught me an important lesson: you don't need much to be used by God. You don't need fancy instruments, formal training, or even a big crowd. You just need a willing heart. God met us in those small rooms just as surely as He met us in sanctuaries filled with people. Songs were sung, prayers were prayed, tears were shed, and burdens were lifted. I watched my grandmother worship with sincerity and humility, and I learned that music, when surrendered to God, can and will be powerful.

> **Just a side note:** If you play the right music in your circumstance, God will run demons and demonic spirits out of your life. Music makes a difference in your day.

As I look back, I can clearly see how my calling in ministry began with my grandma, a piano, a few gospel songs, and a heart devoted to the Lord. My grandmother didn't just teach me how to sing or play; she taught me why we sing. She planted seeds that God would later grow into a lifetime of preaching, singing, and testifying to His faithfulness. For that, and for her quiet, steady example of faith, I will always be grateful.

Many of the sacred moments of my childhood didn't happen in a church building. They happened in living rooms. In those cottage prayer meetings.

I can still see it clearly in my mind, the front room of someone's home, chairs pulled together, people sitting wherever there was space. The furniture was moved back, lamps were turned on, and Bibles were resting on the laps of those dear saints, ready to hear the word of God.

As a child, I didn't speak much at those meetings. But I listened. I listened to the singing, simple songs sung by faithful people who didn't need a choir loft or an instrument to lift their voices. Someone would start with a familiar hymn, and others would join in as they felt led. Then, before long, someone would stand and say, "**I have a testimony**."

That phrase always caught my attention.

They would tell what God had done for them, or how He had touched a family member, or how He had made a way when there seemed to be no way. Their words were not rehearsed, but they were real. After the testimony, another song would follow, sometimes two. Tears were common, and so was joy.

And then, the preacher would preach.

It didn't matter that there were only five or ten people in the room. When that preacher stood, he preached as if a hundred souls were listening. There was no holding back, no easing up because the crowd was small. The Word of God was delivered with the same passion, conviction, and authority as if the house were filled wall to wall.

Those years left an imprint on me, experiences I cannot take back, and experiences I would never want to forget. I watched people sing and be blessed. I watched people preach and be blessed. Everything that happened in those rooms pointed in one direction: all to glorify God.

It's hard to explain the power of an old-fashioned cottage prayer meeting unless you've been in one. And even then, words fall short. There was something sacred about believers gathering not for recognition, not for numbers, but simply to pray, testify, sing, and hear the Word of the Lord.

Those meetings were only part of my story growing up, but they were a significant part. Alongside them were nursing home services and Sunday afternoon radio station services. Each one added another layer, another lesson, another opportunity to serve. Together, they helped shape and define more than 55 years of ministry.

I am grateful for every cottage prayer meeting I attended. I am humbled to have been part of so many live radio broadcast services at the radio station in downtown Wilmington. Those moments taught me something I still carry today, that ministry isn't about the size of the crowd or the place where you stand. It's about faithfulness wherever God sends you.

Looking back now, I realize how closely I watched my pastors and leaders. Men like Johnny Pope, Hovie Pope, George Fowler, and David Casey. Women in leadership like Sister Flowers, Sister Willetts, Sister Lewis, Sister Parker, and Sister Boswell. I watched how they worshiped, how they spoke, and how they handled themselves when no one thought children or young people were paying attention.

And the truth is, we were paying attention.

I assure you that young people today are still watching. Just as I once did, they are observing how leaders act, how they speak, and how they respond in difficult situations. What we do today is shaping the next generation of ministry.

Sun Drops and Square Crackers

One more memory from those early years: I remember going to church with my grandmother so she wouldn't have to go alone, especially on Sunday nights. And the best part of those nights, at least to a young boy, was the treat afterward, those Sunday night Sun Drop sodas and square crackers.

We would sit in front of the Sunset Park Convenience store on Carolina Beach Road and enjoy those simple snacks. I suppose you could call it a "perk" for going to church. Whatever it was, it worked for me.

Years passed, and eventually, I was the one picking up my grandmother to take her to church. And yes, we'd stop by that little store for a Sun Drop and a pack of square crackers.

"The Vessel Called Victory": A Song Conceived During a Crisis, yet Written Years Later

Here's a story and song that I wrote about this incredible saint of God, My Grandma Murleen. Maybe it will make you think of your mother or Grandmother.

Behold, I shew you a mystery; We shall not all sleep, but we shall all be changed, In a moment, in the twinkling of an eye, at the last trump: for the trumpet shall sound, and the dead shall be raised incorruptible, and we shall be changed.
1 Corinthians 15:51-52 KJV

In the early 1980s, I was preaching and ministering, but life was very bumpy. Jenny and I were raising our two young children on a small income, and the enemy seemed determined to trip me up at every turn. Discouragement settled in. Depression followed, and it felt like the devil was winning.

Then came a health crisis.

I found myself in the Intensive Care Unit at Cape Fear Memorial Hospital for fourteen days. My heart would race up to 225 beats per minute, then suddenly drop to 80, only to surge again without warning. The doctors were blunt. They said my heart could literally explode at any moment.

But God, …But God.

In the middle of that frightening season, my brothers, Clyde and Charlie, walked into my hospital room with news that shook me to my core. Grandma had passed away. She wasn't just my grandmother; she was my mentor, my teacher, my spiritual anchor.

As they turned to leave, Charlie suddenly stopped, looked back at me, and said, "Oh, Ray... I forgot to tell you. Just before Grandma passed away, she lifted her hand and waved."

All I could say was, "Wow."

Then something stirred deep inside of me, and I said, "Charlie! Charlie… do you know what she did?" He looked at me, kind of puzzled.

I said, "Charlie…Grandma got on The Old Ship of Zion."

The song "The Vessel Called Victory" wasn't written that day, but in that ICU room, in the shadow of sickness, it was conceived in my heart.

Fast Forward A Few Years: A Time of Searching and Seeking

There are moments in life when you don't need advice, opinions, or explanations; you just need a word from the Lord. This was one of those moments for me.

I entered a seven-day fast, completely shut away from the world. For an entire week, I stayed inside a small mobile chapel; it was just the Lord and me. No distractions. No interruptions.

Reverend Jim Forehand often spoke about "shutting down the machinery." By that, he meant stepping away from everything that makes noise in your life until you can clearly hear from God. I adopted that phrase because it carries deep truth. When you don't know what to do, be still, listen, and hear what God has to say.

Nothing ever catches Him by surprise. Yet many of my mistakes in ministry happened because I moved without seeking His direction. I think way too often, we blame God for our mishaps and missteps when, in reality, we actually acted on our own understanding without getting the nod from God.

I think most preachers know exactly what I mean by that.

We say God sent us here or told us to go there, only to discover the grass wasn't greener on the next hill. This time, however, I truly shut down the machinery with no television, no radio, and no telephone. Jenny knew where I was..., if I was needed.

The fasting ended on a Saturday morning. But before I walked out of that little chapel, I prayed one last prayer:

"Lord, I've talked a lot this week, and I've tried hard to hear from You. Before I go, I just want you to know how much I love you and how thankful I am for all you've done for me."

As I continued to praise Him in the moment, the song that had been conceived years earlier in an ICU hospital room was birthed in my heart and about to be written on paper.

"The Vessel Called Victory" words sprang forth.

A Faith Tested and Proven

Through every season, the Lord has been faithful. His hand has guided my calling and allowed turn-arounds. His Spirit has sustained me in ministry. His voice has spoken life into my heart, birthing even this special song, **"The Vessel Called Victory."**

Since that day in the little mobile chapel, my faith has been tested and tried. There have been seasons when the songs in my heart grew quiet, and the road ahead felt long and lonely. Yet through it all, God has remained faithful. He is a promise keeper. I have been unctioned and anointed by God on more than one occasion to speak words of faith and watch healing and wholeness take place.

That's why it's far too late to tell me God can't heal the sick.
Too late to tell me He can't put broken pieces back together.
Too late to tell me He doesn't specialize in mending broken lives and restoring broken homes.

Too late to convince me that God can't fix what's wrong in your life.

I've already seen too much.
I'm already a witness that God CAN. **Oh, yes, He can!**

And whatever is wrong in your life today, let me testify to you, God can fix it, or God can turn it around.

Humpty Dumpty

I'm reminded of a story Bishop James Leggett told many years ago at Falcon Camp Meeting. He said a teacher was teaching the class the little childhood rhyme about Humpty Dumpty. He told how a little boy was listening intently to the teacher speak the rhyme, how Humpty Dumpty sat on a wall, and Humpty Dumpty had a great fall, how all the King's horses and all the King's men couldn't put Humpty Dumpty back together again.

That little boy raised his hand and asked the teacher: "**If all the King's horses and all the King's men couldn't put Humpty Dumpty back together, why wouldn't somebody just CALL THE KING TO HELP"? CALL THE KING!!!!**

Let me say it again: Whatever is wrong in your life today, let me testify to you... THE KING can fix it; God can turn it around.

This song, "The Vessel Called Victory," is a reminder to me that a song conceived one day, or a promise given one day, will spring forth on another day if we'll stop and listen...and receive.

Thank God for my Grandma...

and

THANK GOD FOR MERCY

MERCY365

PRAYER FOR A GRANDPARENT

Dear God,

Today, as a grandparent myself, I realize the importance of my grandmother's anointing, influence, and gentle coaching in my early life. The prayers she prayed and the words she spoke helped shape the person that I would become.

Now, as a grandfather, I understand that I must also be an influencer to the best of my ability. I must encourage, guide, and lovingly coach the next generation.

Perhaps there is a grandparent now being reminded that their influence can reach far beyond the present moment and touch the lives of future generations.

So, I pray blessings upon a grandma or grandpa as they lovingly intervene for their children and grandchildren. Give them wisdom and compassion. Help them to speak words of life, words of hope, words of peace, and most of all, be a great encourager.

Allow their prayers, their example, and their love to leave a legacy that points the next generation toward You.

This I pray in the name of Jesus Christ.

Amen.

The Vessel Called Victory

CHORUS

My grandma got on a vessel called Victory.
She held up her hand as she waved goodbye.
That vessel departed from all sin and sorrow.
When my grandma got on the old ship of Zion.

VERSE 1

The captain was there—she'd been waiting to meet Him.
She had sung many times of His calling away.
Her mother was waiting—I know they were happy.
When that old ship of Zion took my grandma away.

VERSE 2

I have one desire—oh, that I might meet her.
I remember her prayers so long ago.
She prayed, "Oh dear God, please save all my family.
So when that vessel comes by, they can get on and ride."

CHORUS

My grandma got on a vessel called Victory.
She held up her hand as she waved goodbye.
That vessel departed from all sin and sorrow.
When my grandma got on the old ship of Zion.

CHAPTER FOUR

My Calling into the Ministry

Before I was twelve years old, I felt something stirring inside me. It was a tug, a gentle but unmistakable pull upon my heart, that one day I would stand and preach the gospel. I didn't fully understand it, but I knew a pull was there.

At twelve years old, I had the chance to speak in a Young People's Evening service, which we called YPE back then.
I stood to share what the Lord had put on my heart, but while I was speaking, I noticed a couple of boys in the back snickering.

As a kid, that was all it took. I told myself right then, *if this is what preaching is going to be like, I'm not doing it.*

For the next three years, the calling was still there, but it lived more in my head than in my heart. It wasn't deep yet. It wasn't settled. It was like a seed that hadn't pushed through the soil.

Then, when I was fifteen years old, in the quiet middle of the night, everything changed.

The Holy Spirit woke me, *truly* woke me, and began to deal with my heart in a way that I had not known. I didn't hear an audible voice, but the impression was so real, so strong, so deep that I wept under the weight of it. God was calling me to preach the gospel of Jesus Christ. I prayed and cried and asked God, **"Are You Sure, Lord? Is this really You?"**

Somewhere around two or three o'clock in the morning, I couldn't hold it in any longer. I got up, went to my parents' bedroom, and knocked on the door. Upon opening the door, they were wondering what in the world could be wrong.

Through falling tears, I told them, "I just need to tell you… I'm going to preach. Mom and Dad, I'm going to preach the gospel! I'm going to preach, if I have to preach on a street corner. God has called me to preach."

That moment, early in the morning, marked the beginning of my life's calling.

From that day forward, I have preached the gospel of Jesus Christ. No, I haven't been perfect. I haven't always been on point, and I can assure you that I've made my share of mistakes. But one thing has never changed: the calling that God placed on my life has remained steady. I've never turned from it. I've never regretted it. And I'm grateful, deeply grateful, for that night when the Lord awakened me and gave me the courage to knock on my Mama and Daddy's bedroom door with the news of my calling to preach.

More than fifty years have passed since then. I've seen souls saved, lives changed, hearts healed, and families restored. I've stood in pulpits, sanctuaries, revivals, tents, and on street corners, declaring the good news of Jesus Christ. And through it all, HE has been Faithful.

I learned early on that God doesn't always speak audibly, but unmistakably, He will impress His word upon us if we listen closely.

Son, How Did You Know?

It wasn't an accident or a coincidence. To this day, I believe it was a divine word of knowledge I received from God as a young boy that would help me hear and sense God's assignments in the years to come.

Before I stepped into ministry, I was convinced that God had given me a profound word, one that confirmed His hand was upon my life in a way that neither my family members nor I could deny.

Early one morning, in a vision from God, I saw a clear visual of my brother Clyde Jr. coming home that day. When I woke up that Sunday morning, I told my mother, **"Mama, Clyde Jr. will be home today."**

There was just one problem… **Clyde Jr. was in Vietnam.**

My Mama smiled gently and said, "Son, that's sweet, and I do believe he'll be home soon, but it won't be today."

I simply replied, **"Yes, ma'am, but I know what I saw."**

A Special Homecoming Sunday to Remember

That particular Sunday was a Homecoming Sunday at our church. The Happy Goodman Family were the special guest singers, and anyone who loved Southern gospel music back in the day knows how exciting it was to have the Happy Goodmans.

After the homecoming "Dinner on the Grounds" and while the 2 p.m. Gospel Singing was in progress, my Mama told me she was going home and to ride home with my grandmother after the service.

At about 4:15 p.m., as we turned onto Bordeaux Avenue, I saw my mother walking up and down the street, crying and waving her arms. We didn't know what had happened or was happening until I heard her say, "He's coming home! He's coming home, Clyde Jr's Coming Home!"

In the driveway, she looked deeply in my eyes and asked, "Son, how in the world did you know that your brother was coming home today?" I said, "Mom, I believe God showed me in the night." That's why I couldn't keep it to myself.

The Word from the Lord Fulfilled

My dad had been on a fishing trip that weekend, had come home, and had fallen asleep on the couch. Most other family members (including uncles and aunts) were meeting Clyde at the airport. Dad had absolutely no clue about the Sunday afternoon excitement until about 10 p.m., when my brother **Clyde Jr.** walked through the front door at 101 Bordeaux

Avenue, wearing his Army uniform, and woke him with the news.

Oh, my! The tears, the hugs, the laughter, the disbelief, and the joy, it was a sight to behold. More importantly, even as a young boy, I felt it was a divine confirmation to my family and me that God had indeed given me a word of knowledge. (When I say no one knew, *no one* knew. Clyde Jr. was arriving on a medical pass and had not informed anyone in the family.)

Looking back, that homecoming Sunday became a milestone and a cornerstone moment in my spiritual life, setting the course for the ministry with an assurance that God's calling was upon my life.

THANK GOD FOR MERCY

MERCY365

PRAYER FOR THE CALLED

Dear God,

I pray for the calling upon the life of the one reading these words today.

Open their eyes so they may see clearly the assignment that lies ahead of them. Open their ears to hear your voice of direction. Help them recognize the path that You have prepared and give them the courage to step forward in faith to follow Your assignment.

Prepare them, dear Lord, for every mile of the journey. When the road is smooth, remind them to be thankful. When the road becomes difficult, give them the strength to continue walking in obedience.

Grant them Your mercy when they fall short, Your grace when they feel weak, and Your strength when the journey seems long.

Guide their steps, order their path, and let their life fulfill the purpose You have designed for them.

May they walk faithfully in the calling You've placed upon their life.

In the name of Jesus Christ, I pray.

Amen.

CHAPTER FIVE

My Best Friend Jenny

Together Forever

In 1980, a couple in Blowing Rock asked me if I'd sing at their wedding. I told them I honestly didn't know any wedding songs. They insisted that I sing at their special ceremony. I eventually agreed, but on the condition that they'd allow me to write a wedding song. Once it was written, they approved and appeared to love it. (At least, they said they did!)

TOGETHER FOREVER became the song.

As I began thinking, praying, and writing a wedding song, my mind naturally went to Jenny and our commitment as husband and wife. It was based on our journey, our covenant. With that, the words flowed easily because they were rooted in scripture and grounded in true love. I simply sat down and penned the words that I'll share here, but it's important to understand what this song truly reflects.

Together Forever is a reflection of the promises made with my wife, the very woman God placed in my life to be a helpmate through easy times, stormy times, and some very tough times. Virginia "Jenny" King Faircloth has been an incredible pastor's wife.

We met when she was 14, and I was 17, so in reality, she's been there from the very beginning as we planted and revitalized churches and did whatever needed to be done, even if it meant cleaning toilets. She never complained. She never hesitated. She just served.

An incredible wife.
An incredible mother.

Jenny is a woman of the Word. God's Word!

I've watched her, time and time again, read and study God's Word, and hide it deep in her heart. She's spiritually equipped, not just in knowledge, but in wisdom, grace, and compassion.

And something else about Jenny, she is a giver. She will give the last dime if she believes it will help someone else. I've watched that spirit of generosity in her for many years. It's not something she puts on for show. It's who she is.

Because of her high qualities, this song "Together Forever" was easy to write even in our early years of marriage. It was simply a reflection of God's appointment for her and me.

Over the years, whenever we reach the end of the song, we personalize it for the couple being married, calling their names and making it their song, their moment, their covenant. It has been a blessing to sing so many times at so many weddings over the past 46 years

The heart of the song is simple, and you'll find it in scripture:

What God has joined together, let no man put asunder. (Mark 10:9)

THANK GOD FOR MERCY

MERCY365

PRAYER FOR THE HOME

Dear God,

I pray in this hour in which we are living that marriages would be strengthened and that the home would become what You intended it to be from the beginning.

Lord, bless the home and the sacred institution of the family. Let each household become a place of love, peace, forgiveness, and faith that is pleasing to You and a testimony within the community.

Today, we cancel the assignment of the enemy that seeks to destroy the family unit. We ask that Your healing power would reach even into the home of the one reading these words.

Restore what has been strained. Heal what has been wounded. Renew love, patience, and understanding within their family.

Prove Your power, Lord, by doing a work in their lives. Strengthen their home today and in the days to come, and let Your presence dwell in this home.

This we pray in the name of Jesus Christ.

Amen.

Together Forever

CHORUS
Whatsoever God hath joined together.
Let no man put asunder.
For they're united, united forever.
Love will always, always be.

VERSE ONE
When they leave their father and mother.
And they cling to one another's hands.
They're united, united forever.
Their love will always, always stand.

VERSE TWO
As the years go by, and they both grow older,
And they face the many problems that's ahead,
All the good things will outweigh the bad things,
And love will always, always stand,

CHORUS
Whatsoever God hath joined together.
Let no man put asunder.
For they're united, united forever.
Love will always, always be.

CHAPTER SIX

Down to Night and Nothing

But my God shall supply all your need according to his riches in glory by Christ Jesus.
Philippians 4:19 (KJV)

We had just started our family. I was working at the grocery store on a very small salary. Jenny would catch a job here and there, but mostly she was a new mom taking care of little Ray. It was a season where we were struggling, really struggling, just trying to survive.

One night in our young family life, we were down to nothing.

No oil in the heating furnace. No food in the refrigerator, no baby formula for Ray Jr. I mean… nothing.

It was getting late in the evening, and I remember standing there, overwhelmed, wondering what in the world I was supposed to do. I was giving that job everything I had. I was working hard. But the stress of trying to pay bills and figure out how we'd eat the next meal was crushing.

Some people have never known that kind of pressure, but Jenny and I have lived it. We know what it feels like to hit the absolute bottom.

Not knowing what else to do, I told Jenny, "I'm going to the bedroom. I'm going to read the Bible, and I'm going to pray." Back then, in 1978, I had very few books. But as I walked into that room, I reached up and pulled one of the books off the shelf. I don't remember the title of the book, but I certainly remember what happened next.

I began flipping through the pages… and suddenly $20 bills started falling out onto the floor.

Not one. Not two. But a small stack of them.

By the time I gathered them all up, there was around $200. For us, in that moment, that might as well have been a thousand.

If just one $20 bill had fallen to the floor, that alone would've been a miracle. But God didn't let just one fall; several fell, enough to buy oil, enough to buy food, enough to buy baby formula for our son.

You must understand the life we were living then. We went to yard sales because we couldn't buy anything new. Even though I was a meat cutter, we couldn't afford fresh steaks. We bought the marked-down meat, like the old ribeyes or T-bone steaks that had turned dark in the case and were marked down for quick sale. That's how we survived.

So, when that money fell out of that book, it wasn't just helpful, it was holy. It was God saying, "I see you."

I ran to tell Jenny what happened. And while we were still rejoicing over that unexpected miracle, we heard a knock on the door. Standing there was our dear friend, Brother Thomas Greer, holding two big sacks of groceries. He loved bringing us ginger snaps, and he always brought Irish Spring soap.
That night, he brought exactly what we needed.

Two bags of groceries and about $200 from the pages of a forgotten book.

I remember standing there, holding those groceries and that $200, overwhelmed by gratitude and relief. I knew then, without a doubt, that everything was going to be all right.

Philippians 4:19 says, “But my God shall supply all your need according to his riches in glory by Christ Jesus.” And now, almost fifty years later, I can testify that He has done exactly that.

There have been tight and tough days. There have been late bills. There have been seasons where I didn’t know how God was going to do it. But at seventy years old, I can say with a clear heart: **My God has supplied all my needs, and for that I give Him Praise.**

"I have been young, and now am old; yet have I not seen the righteous forsaken, nor his seed begging bread".
Psalm 37:25 (KJV)

And listen, friend, if He took care of us, He will take care of you.

Lift your head. Hold to your hope and believe God for *your* miracle.

The same God who went before me, before my need with someone placing those twenty-dollar bills in that book, is the same God who will meet you right where you are today to manifest a miracle in your life.

THANK GOD FOR MERCY

MERCY365

A PRAYER FOR SOMEONE WHO'S DOWN TO NIGHT AND NOTHING

Dear God,

We humbly come before You, understanding that all our needs are supplied according to Your riches in glory through Christ Jesus.

For your child, who is reading these words today, I thank you that You care deeply about every need. Lord, just as a parent cares for their earthly child and understands their needs, so You clearly understand the needs of Your children.

I ask that You would supply every need according to Your riches in glory.

Touch this individual today. Provide for them. Strengthen them. Encourage them. Let them know that You see their situation and that You are mindful of their every need in this life.

Supply every need they have, and may there be no lack.

This I pray in the Name of Jesus Christ.

Amen.

CHAPTER SEVEN

Dancing In the Rain

My brother Charlie was a wonderful guy, a singer, a worshiper, and a true gift in my life. After Willie got saved, then Charlie surrendered his heart to the Lord, and before long, he was deep in the church, on fire for God. It blessed me more than words can describe. Charlie loved to sing, especially songs like:

Love will roll the clouds away,
Turn the darkness into day.
I'm so glad I now can say,
Love will roll the clouds away.

He and I spent a lot of time together. He would go with me to the radio stations where I was blessed to broadcast. WPJC, WKLM, and a couple of others. My radio program back then was called ***Gospel Truth***, featuring live gospel singing, testimonies, and praising God. Charlie loved it as much as I did.

We also enjoyed simple pleasures. One of our favorite hobbies was playing and winning at pinball. Yes, pinball! We were young, and Carolina Beach had plenty of arcades and 7-Eleven stores with pinball machines. We could put a dime in a pinball machine and make it last all night. Literally.

One particular night, we played pinball until two o'clock in the morning and still had twenty games banked on that same dime when we left the pinball machine. It was just one of those nights, two close brothers, newly anchored in Christ, having fun and celebrating what God had done in their lives.

Charlie had just gotten saved, and he was hooked on Jesus. I was hooked on Jesus, too. My brother Willie was in church. Jerry would soon follow. Clyde Jr. had professed faith early on. The only two I hadn't yet led to the Lord were my mom and dad, but their time was coming.

(It took a while, but on October 2, 1994, I watched my Mom and Dad walk, hand in hand, down the aisle in the First Pentecostal Holiness Church at St. Pauls, NC, and surrender their lives to the LORD.)

Back to the story with Charlie and me...

It was late, two in the morning, when we left the Carolina Beach fishing pier arcade and decided just to ride around and praise God.

We were in Charlie's Volkswagen, probably a '62 model, and we sang one song after another as we rolled through the quiet Wilmington night. I can't remember all the songs, but I do remember one:

I'm gonna be there.
Oh yes, I'm gonna be there.
Free from every imperfection,
I will never have a care.
I'm gonna be, yes, I'm gonna be there.

Oh yes, I'm gonna be there,

On that resurrection morning, I'm gonna be there.

Charlie was driving, getting happy. I was in the passenger seat, getting happy. I had been through some severe storms, especially with my health, and my family knew it. But God was bringing me out, and that night felt like "victory night" down deep in my soul. Jenny was at home waiting on me, knowing I was with Charlie, knowing we were just enjoying the Lord and each other's company, brothers in the flesh, and yes, brothers in Christ.

Our joy carried us down River Road in Wilmington. Back then, River Road was nothing but a dark, lonely stretch of road by the water. Today it's built up, but in those days, it was woods, river, and quiet.

We rode, sang, and worshiped God. Charlie's driving matched the rhythm of praise, speeding up, slowing down, tapping the brake, giving it gas. He was praising God with the pedals, and I was praising God in the passenger seat.

Then suddenly something rose up in my spirit.

I said, **"Charlie, God wants me to wash my hands."**

He looked at me and said, "Wash your hands? Ray, we're on River Road."

"I know," I said, "but this is spiritual. God's telling me, At Last, At Last, my Past is Past. I've got to wash my hands, symbolizing a new season."

I wasn't joking. I wasn't confused. I meant it with everything in me. When God unctioned me, I took Him literally.

"Charlie, find some water. God wants me to wash my hands."

Charlie didn't know what to do. We were having church in that car, and suddenly I was asking him to find water at 2:00 in the morning on River Road.

But there it was, to my right, a big wet mud puddle on the side of the road. It had rained earlier, providing a puddle of water, and the rain continued to drizzle from the early-morning sky. I opened the car door, and then it hit me, not the rain but a thought. River Road has water…but it also has water **snakes**. **(This Pentecostal Don't Do Snakes!)**

The joy I had in the car shifted quickly as I stepped out onto that dark, damp shoulder of the road. I could feel fear rising up as I tiptoed toward that puddle of water. What had I gotten myself into? I was the one who told Charlie that God wanted me to wash my hands, so now what was I supposed to do?

But then something stirred inside me, raising a Holy boldness, a reminder: *This isn't what **you** said, Ray. This is what **God** said.*

And when God speaks, He keeps His Word. I also remembered His promise in the Bible: that "You shall tread upon serpents and scorpions, and nothing shall by any means harm you" (Luke 10:19 KJV).

If a snake crossed my path, God would take care of that. If there were danger in that puddle, He would cover me. I wasn't doing this for emotions' sake, or to be seen or heard of man. I was doing this in obedience to an unction from the Lord.

Suddenly, my fear turned to… PRAISE.

Before I knew it, I wasn't just washing my hands, I was jumping in that puddle. Water and mud splashing everywhere. I was a muddy mess, but God had brought me out of a mess, and it provoked a shout of praise. I was shouting, praising God, celebrating my deliverance. At Last, At Last, My Past was Past!

I must have looked like the muddy mess I was, but I didn't care. The Holy Spirit had touched me, and I was free from oppression and depression.

Charlie stayed in the car, but he was laughing, crying, clapping, and enjoying every second of it.

That night has lived with me ever since. The night I shouted in a mud puddle, dancing in the rain on River Road.

****

So many people find themselves in the mud puddles of life. The enemy tries to scare them, intimidate them, or make them freeze in fear. But the Psalmist said: (Psalm 23) Though I walk through the valley of the shadow of death, I will fear no evil, for Thou art with me. GOD SAYS, “I AM WITH YOU”.

Even darkness or death can’t stop or silence His presence.

And the same God who met me in that muddy puddle wants to meet you right where you are. He wants to set you free, calm your fears, and break the chains of your past or maybe your present.

Whom the Son sets free is free indeed.
John 8:36 (KJV)

And I can tell you, **I walked away from that puddle of water that night freer than I had ever been in my life.**

THANK GOD FOR MERCY

MERCY365

A PRAYER FOR THE HURTING AND DISCOURAGED

Dear God,

I know what it is to be discouraged. I know what it is to be wounded and hurt, even by my own countrymen, by people I love dearly.

So, today I pray for the discouraged heart and for the wounded soldier who may be reading these words.

Lord, give them the courage, the strength, and the resolve to rise up again and step back into the race. Remind them that You are not finished with them yet.

Encourage their broken heart. Lift their wounded spirit. Send the gentle nudge they need from Your Holy Spirit, so they will know that they are not alone and that their purpose is not over.

Help them rise from the ashes of disappointment and pain, for You have promised to give **beauty for ashes**.

Let that promise be fulfilled in their lives even now. Renew their hope, restore their strength, give healing to their heart and bring sunshine in place of the storm that is passing, and by all means, remind them that their story is not over.

This I pray in the name of Jesus Christ.

Amen.

At Last, At Last. My Past Is Past

written February 18, 2026, while reviewing this story

CHORUS

At Last, At Last. My Past is Past
My name's recorded in heaven
Saved, Sanctified. The Blood has been applied
I'm redeemed. My sins are forgiven.

VERSE 1

I once was lost, but now I'm found.
I was on the road to disaster.
But I heard the Good News of the Gospel.
Now I've found the Road of the Master.

CHORUS

VERSE 2

That stir in your heart that's ready to spark
That pull and the call from the Savior
Conviction within. Redemption from Sin.
It's time to come to the Altar.

CHORUS

At Last, At Last. My Past is Past
My name's recorded in heaven
Saved, Sanctified. The Blood has been applied
I'm redeemed. My sins are forgiven.

CHAPTER EIGHT

This is Your Mission Field

Go therefore and make disciples of all the nations, baptizing them in the name of the Father and of the Son and of the Holy Spirit.
Matthew 28:19 (NKJV)

Do you not say, 'There are still four months and then comes the harvest'? Behold, I say to you, lift up your eyes and look at the fields, for they are already white for harvest!
John 4:35 (NKJV)

The Assignment and God's Favor in Shallotte

In the mid-80s, we moved our membership to the International Pentecostal Holiness Church as a door opened for ministry at the Winter Park Church in Wilmington, North Carolina. The church had asked me to serve as their associate pastor and music director. At that time, Jenny and I also oversaw the children's ministry.

For a little over a year, I worked closely with the pastor.

Then, one night in 1986, while attending a district conference in Sneads Ferry, North Carolina, something life-changing happened. The evangelism director, Rev. D. Chris Thompson, was speaking about planting new churches in strategic areas. He said, "Pray that God will send people to these places."

One of the areas he mentioned was Brunswick County. The moment he said it, something stirred deep inside me. It was more than an emotion; I felt that it was a calling. I knew in my spirit that this would be my assignment. I didn't tell anyone right away, but the pull to respond grew stronger each day.

Two weeks later, I approached my pastor, who was also named Ray (Ray J. Ward), and said, "Brother Ray, I need to talk to you."

Before I could go any further, he said, "You're going to Shallotte."

Surprised, I asked, "How did you know?"

He smiled and said, "I knew when the Shallotte area was mentioned at the Sneads Ferry service that God had touched your heart."

So together, Brother Ray J. Ward, Brother R.L. Downing, and I set out to "spy out the land," just like the 12 Israelites, which included Joshua and Caleb. Except we were looking for a place to plant a church in the Shallotte area.

Around that same time, the pastor of Lettie's Grove Pentecostal Free Will Baptist Church (Brother Maurice Milligan) called me and asked if I would preach a revival at his church. I hesitated.

"Brother Milligan," I said, "I'm getting ready to plant a church in that area, and that might not sit well with some."

However, Brother Milligan responded with a Christlike spirit. "Brother Ray, we're not in competition. We're all on the same team. We want you to come and preach for a week."

That revival turned out to be a powerful time of ministry. Back then, the church had about 25 people, but today it's known as Highest Praise, a thriving congregation with hundreds in attendance.

Every time I drive by and see how God has blessed that congregation, I remember those revival days and how I did my best to encourage those few faithful saints: "You praying mothers, you praying fathers, listen, one day you'll see the fruit of your prayers." And surely, God has honored those prayer warriors.

As we continued our search for a building, we stopped at a mobile home sales lot on Highway 130 (Holden Beach Road) in Shallotte to ask the proprietors if they knew of any available buildings for rent. That simple visit turned into one of the greatest examples of God's divine favor I have ever experienced.

That evening, the phone rang. The man on the other end asked, "Is this Ray Faircloth?"

"Yes, it is," I replied.

He said, "My name is Frank Gales. You came by our mobile home sales lot today looking for a building to start a church. I just wanted to tell you that my wife, Carolyn, and I have heard you preach on WVCB, and I told her that if I ever had a chance to help you, I would."

Frank went on to explain that they were moving their offices into a double-wide soon, which would leave their current building vacant. Then he said something that I could never forget.

"I'd like to let you use our current office building to start a church. No rent. The lights are in my name, so you won't even have a light bill or a water bill. I just want you to open up this church."

It was pure favor from God.

Today, in 2026, if you drive down Gray Bridge Road off Holden Beach Road, you'll see the Harvest Fellowship Church standing strong. Behind the church fellowship hall is a small building that we once used as our fellowship hall and later as a Royal Rangers classroom. It's still there today, a quiet reminder that this ministry began not by human effort, but by God's mercy and grace, certainly by divine favor.

The song "This Is Your Mission Field" was written not long after the church had moved from Holden Beach Road to a mobile chapel less than a mile away on Gray Bridge Road.

During the Christmas season in 1987, a family in the Shell Point area would have gone without Christmas if no one had stepped up to help them.

Our little church came together to gather toys for the children, as well as food, groceries, and supplies for the family. I loaded everything into my car, excited to deliver the gifts, only to discover their house was down a long dirt path off Shell Point Road. I remember the scrapes and scratches on my new car, and I thought, "I should have driven something else."

It was at that moment that the Lord impressed upon me: *Son, this is your mission field.*

*****

On the mission field, there will be scrapes, scars, and you will experience pain as well. I sensed His comfort immediately: It was as if He was saying, *I promise you, Son, I'll pay you back for every scratch on the side of this car. I'll pay you back.*

Now, looking back over the years, I can say with my whole heart, truthfully and unequivocally, God has paid me back many, many times.

After feeling that peace, I went inside the church and wrote the song:

This is your mission field; this is your foreign land.
It is I who called you; you've not been called here by man.

I've called you to this harvest, to bring in all the sheaves.
I've called you to this mission field to tell the world of Me.

I share this song with you today as a reminder: you may be serving in a major city with thousands of people to reach, or you may be in a tiny village with just a few. Wherever God has placed you, that is your mission field. You don't need to cross the sea; you just need to see the Cross.

If you follow God's leading with the great message of redemption through Calvary's Cross, I believe one day you will hear Him say, *Well done, thy good and faithful servant.*

Mercy met me at the Cross. And Mercy met me on the Mission Field in Brunswick County. Everywhere I go, I can depend on God's Mercy…. And YOU CAN, TOO!!

THANK GOD FOR MERCY

MERCY365

PRAYER FOR THE LOCAL AND WORLD MISSIONARY

Dear Lord,

I offer this prayer for the missionary, not only for those who travel across the sea, but for all those who see the cross clearly right where they are, both far and near.

Whether they live in a large metropolitan city or in a small, quiet village, I pray that they will recognize the significance of their calling and the importance of their assignment.

Lord, rekindle the passion You once placed within them. Let the fire of God burn again in their hearts so they may fulfill the assignment You've given them to do.

Remind them that where they stand is their mission field, and the people around them are the ones You have called them to reach. Strengthen them, encourage them, and remind them that their labor in the Lord is not in vain.

May the fire of Your Holy Spirit burn brightly within them as they continue the work of ministry on the Mission field.

In Jesus' Name I Pray.

Amen.

Your Mission Field

Christmas 1987

VERSE 1

Seems so oft I've struggled and given all away,
Then God sends down his blessings,
Assuring me he's here to stay.
Then a word comes from the Father,
I'm so glad that you obeyed,
And when you get to heaven,
It's going to be your payday.

CHORUS

Son, this is your Mission Field. This is your foreign land.
It is I who called you. You've not been called here by man.
I've called you to this harvest, to bring in all the sheaves.
I've called you to this Mission Field to tell the world of me.

VERSE 2

Matthew 28:19 says, "GO and spread the word."
John 4:35 says, "Now's the time to let it be heard."
The problem's not the harvest, it's the laborers who are few.
And Jesus beckons to his church,
It's getting late… What will you do?

CHORUS

Son, this is your Mission Field. This is your foreign land.
It is I who called you. You've not been called here by man.
I've called you to this harvest, to bring in all the sheaves.
I've called you to this Mission Field to tell the world of me.

PART TWO

God's Mercy Upon Others

Just as mercy follows me from season to season, I have also seen it unfold in the lives of others around me. Testimony after testimony of the saving mercy and grace of God being applied.

These stories and songs are a testament to how God's mercy has shown up in friends and loved ones… that I know or have known.

I'm amazed that God will do the work if we'll just be his mouthpiece. If we invite people to come to His house, they won't all come, but some might. You just never know.

Our church has had, for many years, what I call "A sign campaign." We buy yard signs for the congregation and rent billboards along the road to advertise the Church. However, I learned many years ago that signs don't bring people to church; people do. Now, don't misunderstand me, I still believe the sign campaign works, but only because it raises the morale in the church, and that, in and of itself, causes church growth.

Who wants to go to a church with low morale? Not me! I believe the JOY of the LORD is our strength!!! JOY and exciting morale go together. A sign has a 3% chance of bringing someone to Church, but a personal invite has a 95% chance of getting someone to attend as a guest. If we learn how to invite people to church, we can also learn how to invite them to Christ. It must start somewhere with someone.

CHAPTER NINE

"I Came Here to Get Saved!"

I remember a time in Bethel, North Carolina, when I had been out knocking on doors, inviting people to church. While walking through the community, I met a man named Bobby. During the conversation, I invited him to Church.

The following Wednesday night, Bobby showed up at church. That particular Wednesday night happened to be the men's and women's ministry monthly meeting night. The men gathered in one room while the ladies gathered in another.

I noticed right away that Bobby had brought a big Bible to the service, or what he thought would be a service. He sat quietly holding that bible and listening.

At some point during the meeting, whoever was the Men's Ministrics treasurer announced that it was time to collect the Men's Ministries monthly dues. I, too, was new at that church and didn't know what the dues were, but I did know that Bobby wouldn't be expected to pay them. I mean, as far as I knew, it was his very first time being there.

So, I spoke up and said, "I'll take care of his 'Dues'."

The meeting continued, with the men discussing plans, ideas, and things they wanted to do. Honestly, not a whole lot happened that evening beyond collecting dues. Eventually, there was a closing prayer, and everyone began preparing to leave.

As people were walking out, Bobby suddenly spoke up and said, **"Where are y'all going?"**

Someone replied, "Well, it's over with. The meeting is over."

Then I heard what every preacher—every Christian—should want to hear.

Bobby spoke so that all could hear his heart: **"Well, I came here tonight to get Saved."**

Thank God for that BOLD desire!

I wish to God that someone would step out this Sunday or Wednesday with a bold proclamation, "I CAME HERE TO GET SAVED."

Right then, I stepped over to him and said, "Bobby, let's kneel right here."

We got on our knees, and we prayed together. Bobby asked **Jesus Christ to be the Lord of his life**, right there on that Sunday school room floor. No music, no Hammond B3 organ, no official altar call. Just a hungry heart and a willing servant with a made-up mind! That Church was filled with joy that night as they watched a hometown boy come home to Jesus.

That memory has stayed with me. It reminded me that **we never know who is around us**.

Sometimes we rush through our programs, our schedules, and our routines, not realizing that a Ray or a Bobby is sitting right in front of us… Someone who is ready to be saved.

Too often, all it takes is stopping long enough to say, "Would anybody like to give their heart and life to Jesus Christ today?"

Those of us who have grown in the Lord should be equipped enough to step up and say, "Let me help you with that."

*****

A Guide for Soulwinning:

It's like ABC…

1. ADMIT to God that you are a sinner.
2. BELIEVE in Jesus Christ as God's Son.
3. CONFESS your faith in Jesus Christ as Savior & Lord.

<u>Admit</u> That You Are a Sinner.

As it is written, "There is none righteous,
no, not one."
Romans 3:10 (KJV)

You must ask God to forgive you and save you.

"That is thou shalt confess with thy mouth the Lord Jesus, and shalt believe in thine heart..."
Romans 10:9-10 (KJV)

"For all have sinned and come short of the glory of God." Romans 3:23 (KJV)

"Wherefore, as by one man sin entered into the world, and death by sin; and so death passed upon all men, for that all have sinned:"
Romans 5:12 (KJV)

Sin Has an Ending ... It Results in Death.

"For the wages of sin is death."
Romans 6:23 (KJV)

"But God commendeth his love toward us, in that, while we were yet sinners, Christ died for us."
Romans 5:8 (KJV)

When Jesus died on the cross, He paid sin's penalty.

Salvation is a free gift from God to the believer!

" ... the gift of God is eternal life through Jesus Christ our Lord."
Romans 6:23 (KJV)

"For whosoever shall call upon the name of the Lord shall be saved."
Romans 10:13(KJV)

Most Important

Salvation must happen in your head, but to be effective, it must first happen **in your heart**. And when salvation truly happens in your heart, then, when you lay your head on the pillow at night, you'll know, oh yes, you'll know, that you know, that you know, that you've been **born again**. That's A Wonderful Feeling!

THANK GOD FOR MERCY

MERCY365

A PRAYER TO HELP US BECOME AN EFFECTIVE WITNESS

Dear Lord,

I offer this prayer seeking the fullness of Your Holy Spirit in our lives, that we may be equipped with holy boldness.

You said that when the Holy Spirit comes upon us, we will receive power to be witnesses wherever we go. So, Lord, I ask that You give us the unction and the anointing to share our testimony, the power of boldness to tell the story of what You have done for us.

Remind us that there are many people, like Bobby mentioned in this story, who are searching, hurting, and in need of a Savior. They may simply be waiting for someone who will care enough to ask,

"Would you come to church?"
"Would you hear the gospel message?"
"Would you likc to bc born again?"

Give us a boldness we have never known before. Fill our hearts with compassion for the lost and the courage to speak the name of Jesus.

Help us to be faithful witnesses so that many may come to know the saving grace of Jesus Christ.

In the Name of Jesus, we pray.

Amen.

CHAPTER TEN

Meet My Friend, Vince Moore

In July of 2007, Jenny and I were sitting at a table at the Broad Street Café in St. Pauls having a quiet lunch. It was around two o'clock on a Friday when my phone rang. On the other end was my friend, Vince Moore. Vince and I had been close for years— we joked, teased, and cut up like brothers. But this call wasn't like the others.

With a seriousness I had never heard from him before, he said, "Ray… will you preach my funeral?" I laughed at first. "Not today, Vince." But the silence that followed told me this wasn't one of our jokes.

"No, man," he said, voice trembling. "The doctor just came in. He's giving me five days… maybe two weeks to live."

My heart dropped. I asked to speak to Susie, his wife, but when she came on the line, I couldn't get a word out. I handed my phone to Jenny. I was speechless.

Our families shared a bond unlike any other. Jenny loved Susie deeply. We loved their boys, Michael and Kenny. We vacationed together. Opened Christmas presents together. They weren't just friends—they were our family.

But back in those early years—long before 2007—life had taken its turns.

A Friendship Born Behind a Meat Counter

I first met Vince in a meat department. He, too, was a meat cutter. Later, he sang with the Singing Samaritans, alongside Michael and Biney English, Terry Carter, and others. I emceed a lot of those singings, so we saw each other constantly. Our friendship grew naturally— effortlessly.

Back then, Vince was very legalistic. That's what he had been taught. That's the kind of churches he had been raised in. We agreed many times to disagree, and we laughed while we did it. He saw something in one light; I saw it in another. But a true friendship can withstand disagreement—and ours did.

What matters most is this: before Vince left this life, he mellowed. He grew. In my opinion, he moved closer to the heart of Scripture and away from man-made rules and expectations. God softened him, and I had the privilege of watching it happen.

The Long Road to Wilmington

There came a time when Vince grew discouraged, not necessarily with God, but with church, with people, with life. He drifted away. For almost two years, he was missing in action from the church fellowship in Shallotte that he had actually helped me get started.

But he wasn't missing from my heart.

He lived forty miles from my house - one way. And on the days that I traveled to Wilmington from Shallotte, I went the long route. It made no logical sense, since my parents lived much closer, but something in my spirit said, "Go by Vince's house."

Every time I went, he wasn't home. I'd leave a card on the door, little notes of encouragement…reminders that I loved and appreciated him and the family, and that we were praying for them.

I can't tell you how many times I made that trip. Over and over, month after month, for nearly two years.

Then came Christmas Eve 1989

It had just started snowing, a rare event in the southeastern part of North Carolina, and on Christmas Eve at that. The quiet snow was falling when I heard a knock at my door. I wasn't expecting company.

I opened the door, and there stood Vince.
It had been nearly two years since I'd seen him or the family. Vince had lost so much weight that it took me a moment to recognize him.

But before I could speak, he said, with tears in his eyes, "Ray… I got every card."

Every card, every note. Every prayer I had left on that empty porch for nearly two years.

Something happened in that moment. They stepped into the living room, and the kids, Kenny and Michael, with Ray and Melissa began talking and laughing. Susie and Jenny hugged like sisters reunited. It felt like they had never been gone.

Vince wanted to walk over to the church to see how things were going. Snow was falling, Christmas lights glowing. And there, inside Harvest Fellowship Church (the mobile chapel), the Spirit of the Lord came upon him. Vince cried out to God. And let me tell you, nobody cried like Vince cried. He was a tender-hearted man beneath that rough exterior.

And another thing… nobody sang like Vince Moore either. To this day, he's still one of the greatest gospel singers that I've ever heard. One of the reasons I want to go to Heaven is that I believe when I get there, Vince Moore will be leading the choir. I want to hear him lead that heavenly choir.

Coming Home

That night, standing in the church, Vince said, "Ray, I'm ready to get back where I used to be. I'm ready to come home."

And he meant it.

On his knees, he asked Jesus to forgive him for going astray. We prayed together. MERCY WAS IN ACTION!

Later, his family and ours prayed together.
They got rooted and grounded solid in the faith and in the Church. They soon moved back to Shallotte, and Brother Vince became a deacon, then a minister, then a licensed minister in the International Pentecostal Holiness Church.

And when he died, he was pastoring the Evangel Church in Fuquay-Varina, NC.

Vince didn't just come back home; he *came back home running full speed!*

His life proved he loved God with all his heart, soul, and mind. And Susie became a pastor's wife full of generosity, grace, and hospitality.

Ready To Launch Out

Vince wanted to do more than warm a pew; he wanted to *obey* God, and he eventually pioneered a church in Leland before going on to pastor other churches.

On Sunday afternoons, we would travel from Shallotte to Leland, about 25 miles, to help build the Sonlight Pentecostal Holiness Church.

It grew and flourished, then God moved him to other pastorates…and eventually, as already stated, to the Evangel Church.

*****

You need to ask God to put a "Vince Moore" in your life.

Many people would have given up on Vince. *It's too far to drive. He's too discouraged. He's slipping away.*

But something in me refused to let him go. To me, Vince was a wounded soldier. And wounded soldiers don't need abandonment. They need rescue.

In other words: FRIENDS DON'T LET FRIENDS GO TO HELL.

When I opened the door that Christmas Eve, saw the snow falling, and heard those words, **"I got every card,"** I learned something...

It's never too late to rescue the perishing.

Here's my word to someone today: **Go Rescue Your Friends.**

Someone in your life needs rescuing. Someone is slipping through the cracks. Someone is drifting. Someone is discouraged, wounded, feeling defeated.

Please, don't wait. Don't delay.

Don't assume someone else will go. **Go.**
Put the card on the door.
Drive the extra miles.
Take the long route.
Show them how much you care.

In Isaiah 61, the Prophet told us that Jesus would come to bring beauty for ashes, the oil of joy for mourning, and the garments of praise for the spirit of heaviness. He came to turn our darkness into day.

And we, His people, are His hands and His feet.

The one thing that I have learned from all the seminars I've ever attended, which stands out the most, is this: **People really don't care how much we know, until they know how much we care.**

Vince Moore taught me that.

And I pray his story encourages you to reach for those who feel forgotten, wounded, or who have strayed far from home.
Because sometimes all it takes is a card on a door, an extra mile, or one act of love and compassion to turn a runaway church member into a great messenger of God.

My Blessing Is on the Way

"My Blessing Is on the Way" was written in 1987, in the little building where we had just started **Harvest Fellowship Church** in Shallotte. That little storefront wasn't much, but it was full of faith, prayer, and expectation. God was doing something new, even though the journey had already begun with challenges.

I mean, that very first week after the church was organized in January 1987, jealousy raised its ugly head and was already causing trouble. I had to dismiss the church secretary/treasurer for sowing discord.

For a moment, with that kind of start, I honestly didn't know what was going to happen. The church was a baby—an infant—that was suffering. It was an ugly mess for a brand-new church. But God moved, and God blessed, and we made it through that situation.

Weeks later, it was there, in that small storefront church building, that Vince Moore and I completed this song. I had already written a verse based on the life of Job, his trials, his suffering, and his perseverance. Along with that, I had written the chorus: "My Blessing is on the Way."

As Vince and I talked and prayed, Vince began to speak words that stirred my spirit. He said he had heard that *the darkest time of the night was just before the dawn.*

I said, "Vince, that's the verse.... keep writing."

Then he said he had heard that *the roughest time of the storm was just before the calm.*

Again, I said, "Vince, keep writing. This is verse one!"

And the words continued to flow:

And I know one thing, and that it's for sure,
My battles are won when I pray.
So say what you'll say, but I'll tell you today,
My blessing is on the way.

So, yes, Bro. Vince is credited for writing that first verse, but together we blended our voices, our faith, and our testimony into one song.

It was a true collaboration, born out of prayer, hardship, and trust in God.

I remember the very first time we sang that song. I can still see Frank and Carolyn Gales, with smiles and joy on their faces. It was overwhelming to me seeing them, the very ones God used to provide a house of worship with such expression of Praise and Worship to God, singing with the others, "MY BLESSING IS ON THE WAY".

That small congregation, as a new church family, had experienced hardships and some hard knocks as they were getting things started. Yet, in the middle of it all, God sent a word of encouragement through that song.

As we sang with our whole hearts, and I watched Frank Gales stand up, smiling and clapping his hands, rejoicing in the promises of God. The Word of the Lord went forth, not just in the melody of the music, but with mercy in the moment to bring encouragement to the people of God.

That song carried a message then, and it still carries a message today.

I don't know what you may be going through right now, but I do know this: God's will is to bless you, coming in and going out, in the city or in the country, wherever you are. If you will trust in the Lord with all your heart, and not lean on your own understanding, I can assure you of this one truth:

Your Blessing Is on the Way.

THANK GOD FOR MERCY

MERCY365

A PRAYER FOR SOMEONE WHO HAS DRIFTED AWAY FROM HOME

Dear Lord,

Today, I lift up in prayer anyone who may fit the story of my friend Vince Moore, anyone who may have strayed or wandered from the fold.

Lord, give us wisdom to go and rescue the wounded. Help us to search for those who are discouraged, hurting, or feeling forgotten. Fill our hearts with mercy and compassion as we do our best to guide them back home.

Let Your Holy Spirit lead the way. Give us the right words, the right spirit, and the right timing as we reach out to those who have drifted.

And Lord, as people return, when souls come back to You and lives are restored according to Your will, when someone is saved and redeemed by the precious blood of the Lamb, we will celebrate, and we will give You all the thanks and all the praise.

For every life restored and every soul rescued from perishing, you will receive the glory and the honor.

In the Name of Jesus Christ, we pray.

Amen.

My Blessing is on the Way
written with Reverend Vince Moore

Verse One

I heard that the darkest time of the night was just before the dawn.
And I heard that the roughest time of the storm was just before the calm.
But I know one thing, and that's for sure
Our battles are won when we pray.
So, say what you'll say, but I'll tell you today,
My blessing is on the way.

Chorus

Verse Two

Oh, Job was oppressed. His life was a mess.
His fortune and his family were gone.
His wife said, "Curse God and die.
Job said, "Honey, why? My blessing is on the way."

Chorus

My blessing is on the way,
For the Lord is with me to stay,
Let the devil stand clear,
My blessing is near.
My blessing is on the way.

CHAPTER ELEVEN

The Runaway Preacher

Some years ago, when I worked as a Meat market training manager for Food Lion, new store managers would come through my store for six weeks of hands-on training in the meat market. They were about to run their own stores, and part of their preparation was learning the meat market basics—everything from cutting meat to understanding the inner workings of the department.

It wasn't glamorous work, but it mattered. When issues arose later as a store manager, they'd have basic skills for handling the meat department because they had stood behind a real butcher block with a real knife in their hand.

On one particular day, a new trainee arrived. His name was Mark. The music in the market was blaring; Vestal Goodman and other Southern Gospel greats were filling the room with classic harmonies. Back in those days, when I was cutting meat full-time, I loved nothing more than slicing ribeyes, pork chops, or cubing steak while gospel music filled the air. That was my sanctuary. That was my worship space.

As usual, the trainee's first job was slicing fatback or cubing round steak. So, Mark was stationed at the slicer. He was on his way to being a meat cutter. He had a big stack of fatback to work through, but he didn't seem to mind. I could tell he was grateful for the opportunity and excited to be there. And though slicing fatback isn't everybody's favorite job, it's where you begin, and it's where you start learning in the meat department.

I was on the other side of the room, working at a fast pace. Winn-Dixie had trained me well some years earlier at their facility in Raleigh, and eventually, I'd worked my way into management before moving on to Food Lion. I loved the work! I loved the rhythm of cutting meat. But most of all, I loved doing it while praising God.

After a while, I noticed that Mark started slowing down. Then he turned the slicer completely off. I looked over at him just as he looked over at me.

He hesitated, then asked, **"Was that the Happy Goodman Family playing on the radio when I walked in earlier?"**

I didn't think before I responded- it was instant, straight from the Spirit of God. **"You're A Runaway Preacher,"** I said.

The look on his face said everything. He froze. His eyes widened. He hadn't expected that. He had come all the way to Wilmington, North Carolina, hoping to escape anything that reminded him of the presence of God. His grandmother had prayed for him. His family had prayed for him. He thought if he could just run far enough, if he could just get to the coastline, he could outrun the prayers of his family and the conviction in his heart.

But you can’t outrun God.

I didn’t push him. I didn’t preach at him. I simply kept being me, cutting meat, playing gospel music, and worshiping while I worked.

Five weeks went by.

One day, I was at the meat block, singing as I cut meat. I don’t remember the song, but I do remember the presence of God settling in that meat department just as real as if we were in a revival meeting.

Suddenly, I heard a loud thump.

Mark had slammed his knife down onto the table. I thought he was hurt.

“What’s wrong?” I asked.

His voice was shaking. “I can’t take it no more.”

“What can’t you take?”

“I can’t take this conviction. I’m tired of running. I’m tired of feeling what I feel. I’m ready… I’m ready to make it right.”

Right there, two grown men, a meat-cutter trainee and a market manager, knelt on the semi-wet market floor in that meat department. And with the smell of fresh-cut meat around us and gospel music playing overhead, Mark prayed something like, "God… please forgive me. Please restore my salvation. Please come into my heart. Don't take your Holy Spirit from me. I REPENT."

Tears flowed, the presence of the Lord moved, Heaven came down in that cold meat department, and the fire of the Holy Spirit warmed that large processing room.

Not long after that, Mark returned home. He went back to school. And the last I heard, many years ago, Mark, the Runaway Preacher, was preaching the gospel.

*****

God is still looking for Runaways.

The LORD doth build up Jerusalem: he gathereth together the outcasts of Israel. He healeth the broken in heart, and bindeth up their wounds.
Psalm 147:2-3 (KJV)

I want to tell you something, my friend: **God cares about where you are.**

He cares about the runaway child of God.

He cared about the prodigal that day in Wilmington. He cared enough to put a preacher behind a meat counter to meet a young man on the run.

You might be in the same house that you've lived in for twenty years, but spiritually you've run away. You've stepped back from the touch, the call, the presence you once knew. Like Mark, you've tried to drown it out. You've tried to escape it. You've tried to outrun it.

But you can't outrun God… who loves you very much.

If you feel His tug, even as you read this, why not pray this simple prayer:

"Lord Jesus, I can't run from You any longer.
Please forgive me. Restore me, help me. I need Your strength; I need Your touch today. I REPENT."

And He will do as you ask.
Not only will He forgive you, but He will also restore you.

I've told my church this for years, and I believe it with all my heart:

"When God restores you, everybody will know. Even your dog will know that restoration/salvation has come to your house."

Thank God for Mercy for a Runaway Preacher

THANK GOD FOR MERCY

MERCY365

MY PRAYER FOR A RUNAWAY

Dear Lord,

I pray for the child or the grandchild who has run as far as they can, trying to hide from Your presence.

I pray for the runaway preacher, the runaway Sunday school teacher, the runaway singer, "the runaway" who once sang, preached, prayed, danced, and shouted with victory, but somewhere along the way drifted and ran in another direction.

Lord, I ask that You allow them to come to a clear mind with understanding that they'll never outrun Your presence.

Place someone in their path, a preacher, a deacon, a faithful church member, or a friend, someone who will speak with love and compassion and encourage them to turn around and come back home. Lord, I know you could use this very chapter to turn their thinking around.

It's not Your will that any should be lost, but that all should come to repentance.

So today I pray for restorations. I ask You to bring the backslider home and return them to the place You once called them to.

Draw them back by Your mercy and grace so they may fulfill the assignment You have given.

In the Name of Jesus Christ, I pray.

Amen.

The Lord Had Mercy On Me

VERSE 1
A woman drawing from a well,
She was so lost, she was bound for hell.
She met a man at the well that day,
running back to the city,
They could hear her say;

CHORUS
"Mercy, Mercy… the Lord had mercy on me.
The Lord had mercy on me.
Mercy, Mercy… the Lord had mercy,
He had mercy, He had mercy on me."

VERSE 2
You may be lost, lost as can be.
You may have hangups, just like me.
Turn to Jesus, and you can shout with me,
"The Lord had Mercy, He had Mercy on me."

CHORUS
"Mercy, Mercy… the Lord had mercy on me.
The Lord had mercy on me.
Mercy, Mercy… the Lord had mercy,
He had Mercy, Mercy on me.

He had mercy,
The Lord Had Mercy on me."

CHAPTER TWELVE

Spiritual Transmission Failure

The Gordon Knox and Harry Keyhoffer Story

Harry Kehoffer first came to North Carolina to meet Judy, and something remarkable happened. They fell in love almost instantly. It wasn't long before the two of them were married, and Harry began settling into life in a little community called Trap, North Carolina. He was a happy man, grateful for his new life and his new bride, but there was one thing he had left behind. It wasn't a wife; it was his tools.

Harry was a mechanic, and his tools were more than pieces of metal. They were the instruments through which he worked on small engines and all kinds of equipment that God had gifted him the ability to fix. But those tools were still in New Jersey, and without them, Harry couldn't fully step into the work he was trained and talented to do.

One day, our men's ministries director, Brother Gordon Knox, gathered four of us together. With his Ford F-250 hitched to a 16-foot trailer, we left early one morning to retrieve Harry's tools from New Jersey.

When we arrived, it took more than half a day to load everything. The truck and trailer were jam-packed— stuffed full of heavy toolboxes and equipment that Harry had collected over the years.

After hours of work, we began our journey back home and stopped in Woodbridge, Virginia, near Washington, D.C., to get something to eat, knowing we still had many miles ahead. But around five o'clock that afternoon, in the center lane of I-95—right in the peak of Friday traffic—trouble hit. The traffic was starting and stopping until Gordon stopped once, but the truck wouldn't start back up.

The transmission had gone out completely.

Cars were flying by us, horns blaring, people yelling, and several giving what Jed Clampett once called the "California Howdy." Drivers were frustrated and rude, not knowing we were stuck and helpless.

For over an hour, we sat there—four grown men locked inside a dead pickup in the center lane of one of the most heavily traveled highways in America. Traffic was so heavy we couldn't even open the doors. We were stranded, helpless, and watching the world speed past us.

Finally, after what felt like a lifetime, a DOT truck pulled behind us. They stopped traffic long enough for us to hook the trailer to their vehicle and move Gordon's truck off to the shoulder.

Four grown men had been cussed at, yelled at, and given more hand gestures than we could count. The drivers didn't know our situation. They didn't know the transmission had failed. They just saw four men in a truck that wasn't moving—four men "in the way."

What they didn't know was this: inside that stranded truck sat four men who loved the Lord. And right there in the middle of I-95—when we had no idea what to do—Gordon Knox did something I will never forget. He reached behind the seat, pulled out his Bible, opened to the Sunday School lesson for the coming week, and began to teach.

Think about that for a moment.

Four grown men, sitting in a broken-down Ford F-250 in the middle of one of the busiest interstates in America, listening to the Word of God.

That's why this story must be told.

Because when Gordon didn't know what else to do, he turned to Scripture.

And in doing so, he taught us a lesson none of us would ever forget.

Trust God in the Breakdowns.

There are times in life when our spiritual transmission breaks. It's not that the truck has no value. It's not that the engine won't run. It's simply that it won't move.

Somebody reading this may feel exactly that way. You want to sing. You want to preach. You want to serve the Lord.

But suddenly you find yourself stuck right there in life's Friday evening traffic with no way out and no idea what to do.

But I'm telling you that **Jesus is about to pull up behind your vehicle. He is about to give you direction. He is about to make a way.**

Because the story wasn't over.

While we were standing in the median—four confused, tired men waiting for a miracle—a well-dressed lady pulled up behind us.

She stepped out of her truck and said, "I'm a truck driver. I've just come from a funeral in New York, and I'm heading to Richmond. Looks like you boys could use some help."

We looked at each other in disbelief.

Within minutes, she had our trailer hooked to her truck. And the next thing we knew, four grown men were climbing into her pickup. I can't remember whether her truck was a Ford or not—but I will never forget her kindness.

She hauled that 16-foot trailer all the way to Richmond, where our church member, Billy Mulder, met us and took us the rest of the way home.

You talk about God providing. You talk about God sending help. You talk about a ram in the thicket— He sent one that day on I-95.

No matter what you are facing today, don't give up. God knows exactly where you are. He knows how to send the right person at the right moment. And He will.

We were stranded in the center median of I-95 in Woodbridge, Virginia—just outside the nation's capital—with no clue what to do. But by the wee hours of the morning, we were back home. God had made a way.

Harry Kehoffer got his tools. Gordon Knox got his truck to the transmission shop. And the whole crazy day became a memory.

A memory worth telling. A memory I call **the Miracle on I-95.**

God has a miracle on the road you're traveling today.

MERCY ON THE HIGHWAYS OF LIFE

THANK GOD FOR MERCY

MERCY365

PRAYER FOR SOMEONE IN A SPIRITUAL BREAKDOWN

Dear God,

I am aware that many people find themselves stuck right in the middle of religious freeways. There are praises all around them. There is worshiping of God and rejoicing happening everywhere they look.

Yet somehow their own spiritual transmission is broken, and they find themselves simply going through the motions.

I ask that You would send help from heaven. Let the angels of the Lord pull up behind them and beside them, like a DOT truck on the side of a busy highway. Let Your Spirit make it known that help is on the way.

Even now, Lord, let someone reading these words feel hope rising in their heart and know that help is on the way.

I declare that the spiritual transmission that once worked so well but has been worn down by the miles and burdens of life is about to be restored. May the calling of God be rekindled and refired within the hearts and lives of the readers.

Breathe fresh strength into their spirit. Renew their passion. Restore their joy.

Let it be so, even now.

In the name of Jesus Christ, I pray.

Amen.

GOD'S NOT FINISHED WITH YOU YET

CHORUS

God's not finished with you yet,
God's not finished with you yet.
If you'll only believe, I believe you'll receive,
Because God's not finished with you yet.

VERSE

Have you cried through the day?
Does it seem there's no way?
Oh God's not finished with you yet!
Keep your eyes on the prize, and look up to the skies,
Because God's not finished with you yet.

CHORUS

God's not finished with you yet,
God's not finished with you yet.
If you'll only believe, I believe you'll receive,
Because God's not finished with you yet.

CHORUS

God's not finished with you yet,
God's not finished with you yet.
If you'll only believe, I believe you'll receive,
Because God's not finished with you yet.

CHAPTER THIRTEEN

"That Was Me One Day"
Deedy White's Testimony

We had just attended my brother William's funeral at Scotts Hill Baptist Church in October of 2024. As we walked toward the car, I saw our friend Deedy White. He had made the trip all the way from Shallotte just to support our family. As my wife and children thanked him for the distance he had traveled and for his love and prayers, Deedy kept steering the conversation back to the service we had just experienced.

My brother William was saved to the bone. He knew he was going to Heaven, and he wanted to take as many people with him as he possibly could. After salvation, he had a story to tell… and he wasn't ashamed to share it. Anywhere, To anybody, At any time.

The pastor that day, Phil Ortego, spoke about how lost we all are without Christ. He spoke honestly of his own journey to salvation, how he discovered that religion, goodness, or tradition alone would not save a man. It must be Jesus. It must be mercy and grace, and it must be personal.

Standing there in that parking lot, Deedy recalled his own journey. He testified that Pastor Landis Lancaster had preached a message many years earlier that brought conviction and then led to his conversion. For years, Deedy had assumed he was automatically saved. But the Holy Spirit showed him that we must be born again. And when Deedy and Jean got saved… they got good and saved!

Referring to William's homegoing service, Deedy kept saying over and over again, **"That was me one day."** He said it with tears of gratitude. "I was lost and didn't even know it…but Jesus saved me."

And as he described his conversion there in that Scotts Hill parking lot, he wept with joy that salvation had come to him. Again, with emphasis, and pointing back to the message we had just heard about being so lost, then gloriously saved, he said, **"That was me one day."**

The truth is, we were all lost and undone without God or His Son until we heard a gospel message that we could be free from the burden of sin. Salvation requires more than believing we're "good people." It requires redemption. It requires repentance. And it requires the shed blood of Jesus Christ.

William knew it. Deedy knew it.

And God wants everyone to know it.

THANK GOD FOR MERCY

MERCY365

A PRAYER FOR SALVATION

Dear Lord,

Today I pray for someone who may be passing by these pages, someone who has yet to ask You to be their Lord and Savior.

Just as it was with Willie and Deedy, and just as it was in my own personal life, we had to come by the way of the cross. We had to ask Jesus to become the Lord of our lives. We are none saved automatically. WE MUST BE BORN AGAIN.

So right now, I pray that the Holy Spirit would draw, beckon, and gently pull on the heart of someone reading these words. Give them the courage to surrender their life to Jesus Christ.

And if that person is ready for the journey of eternal life, allow them to pray a simple prayer like this:

"Lord, I know that I am lost and that I am a sinner. And I also know that I need a Savior, and I believe that Jesus Christ is that Savior. Please come into my life, forgive me of every sin, and make me new and whole through the blood you shed for me on the cross.

I believe that Jesus is the Christ, the Son of the living God. From this day forward, my life belongs to You."

Lord, I thank you that when someone prays that prayer with sincerity and faith, because their life will never be the same, never, never, never be the same... in Jesus Name.

Thank You for the miracle of salvation.

Amen.

That Was Me One Day

inspired by Deedy White
after my Brother William's Funeral

VERSE 1

On the outside, looking in, my life was filled with sin.
There was no real peace within. That was me one day.
Then I heard Amazing Grace. I accepted Christ by faith.
All my sins were washed away. That was me one day.

CHORUS

That was me one day. That was me one day.
I shall never forget. My sins were washed away.
Yes, that was me one day, and I'm not ashamed to say,
My night was turned to day. That was me one day.

VERSE 2

Climbing up to see, but the Savior knew my need,
Zacchaeus was just like me. That was me one day.
Drawing near to Christ, He went home with me that night.
The wrong was turned to right. That was me one day.

CHORUS

That was me one day. That was me one day.
I shall never forget. My sins were washed away.
Yes, that was me one day, and I'm not ashamed to say,
My night was turned to day. That was me one day.

PART THREE

GOD'S MERCY FOR HEALING

I was given a front-row seat to see God's mercy as it transformed lives around me. I've watched it show up in hospital rooms, during altar calls, in quiet prayer meetings, and in moments when someone thought all hope was gone.

I've seen lives change right in front of me.

I've seen people run towards God, while I've seen others try to run away. And yet, His mercy remained steady.

I've witnessed God, in His loving-kindness, draw backsliders back to Himself. His mercy has never been fragile. It never expires. It did not withdraw when we stumbled. It waited. It worked. It restored. And it was renewed with every sunrise.

Not only in restoration, but I have also experienced and witnessed His mercy firsthand through divine healing. That's what this small chapter is all about. Healing!

Healing does not always arrive instantly or without pain. Sometimes it comes suddenly, though expectantly miraculously. Sometimes it unfolds progressively. Sometimes our healing comes through medicine and skilled hands blessed and anointed by God. And then, for clarity, if we live long enough and the Lord tarries, our ultimate healing will come as God, in His sovereign wisdom, calls us to our heavenly, eternal home. As Jesus showed us firsthand, the grave is not the end, just the beginning of eternity.

Even then, as we stand before our Heavenly Father, the Mercy of God through His Son, Jesus, who is the propitiation of our sin, will make up any lack for the believer who could never enter heaven based on their name, fame, or wealth.

In this section, I share a very small portion of the stories and songs I wrote about the healing mercies God showed me in seasons of sickness and pain. I hope to share more testimonies soon. Healing mercies have sustained me in the past and continue to sustain me today.

This is a synopsis of my personal testimony behind the song “I’m Healed by the Power of God,” born from a moment when God intervened in an unmistakable way. You will also hear the heart behind “Healings Happening,” a declaration that God is still moving, still touching, and still restoring.

This section stands as my affirmation of **Divine Healing**

Instantaneous, progressive, medicinally, and ultimately. However God chooses to heal… HE IS THE HEALER!!

Above all, this is my testimony of faith that

God’s Mercy Still Heals the Sick.
God’s Mercy Still Sustains and Gives Joy.
God’s Mercy Still Keeps Me on My Worst Day.

THANK GOD FOR MERCY

MERCY365

CHAPTER FOURTEEN

Divine Healing

Who has believed our report? And to whom has the arm of the Lord been revealed? 2 For He shall grow up before Him as a tender plant, And as a root out of dry ground. He has no form or comeliness; And when we see Him, there is no beauty that we should desire Him. 3 He is despised and rejected by men, A Man of sorrows and acquainted with grief. And we hid, as it were, our faces from Him; He was despised, and we did not esteem Him.4 Surely He has borne our griefs and carried our sorrows; Yet we esteemed Him stricken, Smitten by God, and afflicted. 5 But He was wounded for our transgressions, He was bruised for our iniquities; The chastisement for our peace was upon Him, and by His stripes we are healed.
Isaiah 53: 1-5 (KJV)

Who Himself bore our sins in His own body on the tree, that we, having died to sins, might live for righteousness, by whose stripes you were healed.
1 Peter 2:24 (KJV)

I Submit, somewhere between **Isaiah, chapter 53**, and **First Peter, chapter 2**, something supernaturally happened.

Isaiah said it would happen, and Peter confirmed it. We would be healed, we are healed. It's just that simple!

The same remedy for our sin-sick souls is the same remedy for the healing of our broken bodies.

Furthermore, I will proclaim with all that is within me that should the Lord never heal me of another sickness, I am still a personal witness to his healing touch. Folks, I have seen too much, and I have personally witnessed and experienced too much, for anyone to try to convince me that healing was only for yesterday or limited to the early Church.

Healing is not a theory to me. It is not secondhand information. It is not something I just happened to read about in a commentary. It is something I have watched with my own eyes, felt in my own body, and lived out in my own journey with God.

What Isaiah prophesied, Peter proclaimed, and what the Word declared, the Lord performed.

As a young boy, I can remember attending revival meetings, tent meetings, church services, and special gatherings where **healing** was very much a part of what I witnessed. In those days, I didn't analyze it or question it—I simply saw God move, and it marked me for life.

One memory in particular has never left me.

My great-aunt was bound to a wheelchair. Every time I ever saw her, she was in that chair. I never asked why. I never inquired whether it was paralysis, arthritis, or something else. I just knew one thing—my great-aunt did not walk.
One night, during a meeting with an evangelist at a large meeting hall, I watched as that preacher prayed for her.

He said, "God is getting ready to do something supernatural right now."

I was glued to that moment—the preacher, the wheelchair, my great-aunt. I watched closely, wondering what was about to happen. As he prayed, he took her by the hand—and she stepped out of that wheelchair.

The people who knew her best—better than I did—began to rejoice, clap, and worship, because they knew without a doubt that a supernatural, divine intervention had just taken place.

But that wasn't the end of the story.

To my amazement, the preacher who had prayed for her sat down in the wheelchair—and my great-aunt pushed him all over the building while people sang, clapped, and worshiped God.

That was one of the earliest miracles I can personally testify to. And there have been many others along the way.

Another miracle involved a man who became a dear friend, Marshall Heath, who has since gone on to be with the Lord. The first time I ever saw Marshall, he, too, was bound to a wheelchair. Years earlier, in 1976, he had taken the swine flu shot, and an adverse reaction left him paralyzed from the waist down.

I didn't know him, his story, or his actual condition. But in a Sunday night service in the early 1980s, I looked at him and said, "You're going to be walking within 24 hours."

That's all I knew to do, just say what came out…. in faith.

As I turned and walked back toward the pulpit, my human mind kicked in. *What if he doesn't walk?* But then the Lord spoke to that young preacher's heart, *But what if he does?*

The next morning, at ten o'clock, my phone rang. On the other end, all I could hear was, "Hallelujah! Hallelujah! Hallelujah!"

He said, "I got out of bed, and I'm walking. I have my strength. I am healed."

A few hours later, Marshall came to see me and walked all around the automobile, testifying about what God had done.

There are many more stories I could tell, but I can also tell you this: **God healed me.**

The story and the songs, "I'm Healed by the Power of God" and "Healing's Happening" are testimonies, reminders, declarations that God did… and He can do it again!!!!!!

If God did it for me,
God will do it for you.
To God be the glory,
I'm healed by the power of God!

PRAYER FOR HEALING

Dear Lord,

As a child, I can remember my grandmother laying her hand on my fevered brow and praying a simple prayer in the name of Jesus: *"Touch my boy."*

Now, with that same authority and that same anointing, I ask for healing for someone who is reading this page right now. As Your anointing rests upon these words, may healing begin to flow.

Lord, let there be healing right now for the reader.

God, I thank You that You were wounded for our transgressions. You were bruised for our iniquities. The chastisement of our peace was upon You, and by Your stripes we are healed.

So let that healing manifestation take place right now.

In Jesus' name,
Amen.

CHAPTER FIFTEEN

Healed By the Power of God

Again I say unto you, That if two of you shall agree on earth as touching any thing that they shall ask, it shall be done for them of my Father which is in heaven. [20] For where two or three are gathered together in my name, there am I in the midst of them.
Matthew 18:19 (KJV)

He heals the broken-hearted and binds up their wounds.
Psalm 147:3 (KJV)

In 1989, I developed an unusual growth on my right side, near my lower back. At first, it was small, but it kept growing day by day. Only two people knew about this medical issue — my wife, Jenny, and a coworker I carpooled with each day to the Southport CP&L Nuclear Electric Plant.

The three of us entered into an agreement of faith, praying together and believing that God would heal me and remove this unwanted growth. Our prayer of agreement continued for months. Even as the growth increased in size, we kept bombarding Heaven for a miracle.

Every day, often several times, I would lay my hand on that growth — starting each morning in the shower — and I would curse it at the root, commanding it to die and vanish. Days turned into weeks, weeks into months. Still, there was no visible change. Yet I refused to give up. I kept believing, kept agreeing, and kept confessing God's promises — speaking the things that were not as though they were.

Looking back now, I am so thankful that I didn't quit. I pressed my way to a miracle. It didn't happen the first time I prayed, and it wasn't instantly removed when I first noticed it — but when God moved, it happened instantly.

The Miracle

On New Year's Eve, December 31, 1989, our church, Harvest Fellowship in Shallotte, North Carolina, held a New Year's Eve service — a night filled with prayer, praise, and thanksgiving. The church was young, united, and growing. The Spirit of God was strong, and no one seemed to want to go home. The service carried into the early morning hours of January 1, 1990, ending around 2:00 a.m.

1989 had already been a year of great blessing. Harvest Fellowship Church had been newly organized, the worship center completed, and we were seeing miracles almost weekly. But another miracle was about to unfold.

I had to be at work in Southport by 6:00 a.m., which meant barely an hour of sleep. At 4:00 a.m., I got up, showered, and began preparing for a ten-hour workday. As always, I placed my right hand on that growth and spoke words of faith, declaring healing in the name of Jesus. It was still there — but I still believed.

By 5:00 a.m., we were on the road, rejoicing and talking about the incredible service we had just experienced. I didn't know it yet, but that day would be unforgettable.

In my pocket, I carried small slips of paper with Scriptures to build my faith throughout the day:

James 5:15 – *"And the prayer of faith shall save the sick, and the Lord shall raise him up; and if he have committed sins, they shall be forgiven him."*

3 John 2 – *"Beloved, I wish above all things that thou mayest prosper and be in health, even as thy soul prospereth."*

Jeremiah 30:17 – *"For I will restore health unto thee, and I will heal thee of thy wounds, saith the LORD."*

Philippians 4:19 – *"But my God shall supply all your need according to his riches in glory by Christ Jesus."*

…and many more verses that affirmed God's healing power.

The Moment of Healing

My morning assignment at the nuclear plant began at 7:00 a.m. As a fire watch attendant, I was stationed in the center of the facility — a role that required knowledge of safety protocols in the event of an emergency.

At 7:00 a.m., I reached back as I had done countless times, placing my hand on the growth to declare it healed. But this time it felt different. I checked — was it here? Was it there? No. And then I realized: **the growth was gone**. Between the morning shower at 4:00 a.m. and just a few minutes ago, it had completely dissolved. Vanished. **Gone!**

I could hardly contain myself. I shouted, "I'm healed! I'm healed by the power of God!"

Like the lame man who leaped for joy in the temple, I leaped, shouted, and praised God. My co-worker, Mike, in the adjacent room, witnessed my excitement.

I pushed open the door to him — not with my hands, but with my foot — and it slammed wide open with a loud bang.

Mike's eyes grew wide. "What happened?" he asked.

"It's gone!" I said. "The growth — it's gone! God did it! He healed me!"

We both rejoiced. Months of prayer and faith had produced a miracle. That morning, I began writing a song to testify about what God had done.

The song… "I'm Healed by the Power of God"

By 9:00 a.m., the song was taking shape. The chorus came first.

I'm healed by the power of God,
I'm healed by the power of God.
Yes, I've got the victory,
Since Satan's army had to flee,
My strength has been restored,
Praise God forevermore,
I'm healed! Oh yes, I'm healed,
I'm healed by the power of God.

Verse one followed, inspired by the healing of the lame man in Acts 3 and the power of Christ to restore both body and soul. By the end of the day, the song was complete with two verses giving a living testimony of divine healing.

Faith That Continues

Some say miracles were only for the apostles and the early Church. I beg to differ. We are living in what I call "Acts 29" — the continuation of God's miraculous work today.

The New Testament is filled with benedictions — except in James and Acts. I believe that's no accident. God's plan for signs, wonders, and healings is ongoing. His Word has not changed. What He did for one, He can and will do for all who believe.

Another Healing Testimony

Years later, after serving as Lead Pastor at St. Pauls Life Center Church, I experienced another healing. For over a year and a half, I suffered excruciating pain running down my right leg, a result of a failed back surgery.

One ordinary Sunday night, during worship, I lifted my hands and was instantly healed. No fanfare. No guest evangelist. Just God moving as His people worshiped. The pain was gone.

Once again, I declared: "I'm healed by the power of God! Oh yes, I've got the victory! My strength has been restored — praise God forevermore! I'm healed!"

A Call to Faith

It's too late for anyone to tell me that God cannot do miracles today. Faith in action continues to bring healing, restoration, and victory. The testimonies in this chapter — the growth removed, the pain healed — are living proof.

May the same power touch your life now. Receive it in faith. **Be healed by the power of God! In Jesus' name, Amen.**

THANK GOD FOR MERCY

MERCY365

ANOTHER PRAYER FOR HEALING

Dear Lord,

Your Word asks the question, *"Who has believed the report of the Lord? And to whom is the arm of the Lord revealed?" Isaiah 53kjv*

Your Word declares that Jesus was wounded for our transgressions and bruised for our iniquities. The chastisement of our peace was upon Him, and by His stripes we are healed.

Your servant Peter later declared that **by His stripes we were healed**, reminding us that somewhere between the promise of the Old Testament and the fulfillment of the New Testament, something marvelous happened. The atonement for our sins and sicknesses was provided, and the price was paid, not only for the salvation of our souls, but also for the healing of our bodies.

Lord, somebody needs you; somebody is believing for a healing to take place. They have heard the testimony of what You have done in my life, and I believe that what You have done for me, You can also do for others.

So I ask You now, Lord, let it happen today. Let a miracle take place even now.

Thank You for Your healing touch. Thank you for bringing strength to the weak and healing to those who are afflicted in their bodies and minds.

We speak healing in the mighty Name of Jesus Christ.

Amen, amen, and amen.

I'M HEALED
(By the Power of God)

Written January 1, 1990

CHORUS

I'm healed by the power of God.
I'm healed by the power of God.
Oh, yes, I've got the victory, since Satan's army had to flee.
My strength has been restored. Praise God forevermore!
I'm healed! Oh yes, I'm healed! I'm healed by the power of God.

VERSE 1

A lame man by the gate had suffered many years.
With his cup, he asked for alms as Peter and John came near.
It won't the normal talk when Peter said, "Let's walk."
Then he got right up in Jesus' name,
He was healed by the power of God.

CHORUS

VERSE 2

The stripes upon his back,
They were placed for our disease.
The blood flowed from his side. To set every Sinner free.
For your body, for your soul, He's the answer. Yes, I know,
So be healed. Be healed by the power of God.

CHORUS

CHAPTER SIXTEEN

Healing's Happening

After bilateral knee replacement surgery in 2017, followed by bilateral knee revisions in 2018, and then another set of bilateral knee revisions in 2019, it's safe to say I went through some very difficult seasons with my knees. Even today, they are not perfect, but they are better. And for that, I am thankful. I can walk, and I don't take that for granted.

After the surgeries in 2017, I was stepping out of the car, returning to the rehab facility less than a week after the first surgeries, when a man behind me kept saying, "Man, you sure are moving good. Look at you, look how good you're moving."

I was not amused, and I didn't feel like joking around. This man was behind me; I couldn't see him, but I was thinking, *He doesn't know what he's talking about. He doesn't know the pain that I'm in.*

Then, I turned around and looked, and there he was, an elderly gentleman…sitting in a wheelchair…with no legs.

Stunned and ashamed, all I could say was, "Yes, sir, I'm moving really good, thank you, Sir."

And that second, I realized there's always somebody nearby who's worse off than I am.

Seems that after the last surgery in 2019, the left knee was the hardest of all to recover from. There was no strength and no feeling. I would sit there helpless, praying and crying, asking God to restore strength to my left leg.

I prayed. And people prayed with me.

I remember one particular day after a special time of prayer. I tried again, and this time, I was able to lift my left leg just a little. Maybe half an inch. Not much at all.

But it was movement. It was movement.
It was a miracle taking place.

Right there, in that moment, something rose up in my spirit, and I began to say out loud, "Healing's happening. Healing's happening." And then these words came: "That's what happens when Jesus comes in the room."

Every time I said it, I lifted my leg that same small amount, half an inch at best, but I kept saying it anyway: "Healing's Happening." Before I even realized it, I had written a song:

Healing's happening—
That's what happens when Jesus comes in the room.

That's where this song was born.

And I want to say this to you: you may be going through a struggle right now. You may feel stuck. You may feel like you can't get past the situation, except maybe by half an inch.

But if you're a half inch further than you were yesterday, hear me clearly:

Healing's happening.
Expect God.
Trust God.
Believe God to take the miracle to total completion.

Today, I'm able to walk without a cane or a walker. Yes, my knees still crack and pop, but they're steady enough to carry me across the room. And I know, without question, that God has touched me and helped me through these years.

To God be the glory.

And for you, right where you are…*healing's happening.*

THANK GOD FOR MERCY

MERCY365

ANOTHER PRAYER FOR HEALING

Dear Lord,

We know that You are able to heal instantly and set the captive free. But we also understand that sometimes healing is progressive. Sometimes it does not happen in a single moment.

So Lord, give us the patience to wait upon You and the faith to trust You even when we see no immediate movement, even with our faith applied. Help us not to doubt.

Help us to understand that healing is still happening when we remain faithful and continue to trust You, no matter how healing arrives.

Remind us that healing may come little by little.

So, I pray today that someone will experience Your healing power. Allow them to testify and sing with confidence in the hours and days to come, *"Healings Happening."*

For that's what happens when Jesus comes into the room.

Thank You, Lord, for Your healing touch.

In the Name of Jesus Christ, I pray.

Amen.

Healing's Happening

CHORUS
Healing's happening, healing's happening,
That's what happens when Jesus comes in the room.
Healing's happening, healing's happening,
Oh, I know, yes, I know my healing's coming soon.

VERSE 1
Are you weary? Is your life dreary?
Does it seem that God's not really there?
Let me assure you, He cares for you.
He hears your cry and sees your many tears.

CHORUS

VERSE 2
At the waters in Bethesda
Lies a man who could not move.
But Jesus healed his feeble body.
What He's done for others, He can do for you.

CHORUS
Healing's happening, healing's happening,
That's what happens when Jesus comes in the room.
Healing's happening, healing's happening,
Oh, I know, yes, I know my healing's coming soon.

Part Four

God's Mercy Brings Celebration and Praise

I've got a reason to praise God. I've got a reason to shout and celebrate.

The more I look back over the years, the experiences God allowed me to witness, the miracles I have seen, the tears I have shed, the trials I have endured, the more I recognize a steady thread running through it all.

Mercy was there before I recognized it.

God's steady hand of mercy was always present. It never grew weary. It never withdrew. It never failed.

Rejoicing in God's merciful goodness does not mean pretending that pain, suffering, and grief are not real. Rejoicing in the Lord means understanding that through it all, God remains faithful. It comes from realizing He never let me fall beyond His reach.

Part Four (God's Mercy Brings Celebration and Praise) reflects on the faithfulness of God. These were songs born from a grateful heart. Songs that rise not because life has been easy, but because redemption still sets the captive free.

From "The Lord Is Worthy of My Praise" to "Glory to God in the Highest," every lyric carries one message:

Praising God is what we do for what He Has Done for us.

God’s Mercy gives me a reason to praise.
God’s Mercy gives me a reason to rejoice.
And His Mercy gives me a reason to celebrate.

LET’S CELEBRATE!

CHAPTER SEVENTEEN

The Lord Is Worthy of My Praise

A Celebration for a Great Man of God

One of the sweetest, most soul-stirring homegoing celebrations I have ever attended took place in Greenville, South Carolina, for Bishop Dr. Ronald S. Carpenter Sr. On Tuesday, September 25, 2012, Rev. Danny Harris and I traveled the long road to be part of this breathtaking Celebration of Life. He was our Bishop. He was our Pastor. He was a modern-day mover and shaker of the Pentecostal faith. Hundreds of missionaries, pastors, conference leaders, and denominational officials from around the world gathered that day. Thousands more tuned in online to honor a man they deeply respected and loved.

Bishop Carpenter was perhaps the most compassionate and passionate man of God I ever met. He preached without notes, but with such fervor that he often carried two or three handkerchiefs to wipe his tears. Every testimony that day—whether humorous or deeply moving—reminded us of his impact. His son, Ron Carpenter Jr., ministered powerfully as he shared memories of his father that touched every heart.

“A Gotta-Go-To-Samaria Kind of Leader”

During Bishop Carpenter’s sickness and again at his passing, my mind went back to some years earlier, when he and Bishop Danny Nelson came to the parsonage in St. Pauls, North Carolina, to present the Antioch Award, an honor given to pastors planting multiple churches.

That evening, I was very sick with pneumonia. I could not attend the Evangelism service. They could easily have handed the plaque to my wife and gone on to fellowship at a restaurant like most people, especially preachers do.

But not Bishop Carpenter.

He insisted on coming to my home personally, into that parsonage, so that he could pray for me.

Such compassion has never and will never be forgotten. That was who he was, always willing to go to Samaria or wherever the need was.

A Preacher’s Preacher

Bishop Carpenter had the unique ability to say more in his opening remarks than most preachers deliver in a month of sermons. Everything he said carried weight, relevance, and anointing. He was truly a preacher’s preacher and a pastor’s pastor.

One of his sermons would eventually inspire the song, "**The Lord Is Worthy of My Praise.**"

The Story Behind the Song

In a memorable message at a Falcon Camp meeting, Bishop Carpenter told the story that had happened at an Evangelism USA meeting in Atlanta, where he had been asked to speak. A church group had attended and brought their choir. According to the Bishop, the pastor and her choir were expressive. VERY expressive. Very "Pentecostal" expressive. Meaning, they had church!

He continued, explaining that some of the attendees seemed uncomfortable with the exuberance of that pastor and her church's praise team. He told how they concluded, and it was time for him to be introduced to bring the evening message.

He told us in that camp meeting message that the person introducing him offered what sounded like an apology for what had just been presented. It was something like, "That's not what Bishop Carpenter had in mind for these services." Now, that's not verbatim, but it's close. And in a moment, I'll tell you why I know it's close.

He explained that when he stepped to the podium, he said to the audience, "**That's exactly what I had in mind for these services**."

Then he said he immediately called the pastor and her singers back to the platform to sing again, and they did so with even *greater* expressive praise and anointing.

As he continued, Bishop Carpenter shared that the pastor told the people they knew how to be quiet, how to sit down, and how to be dignified. Then he explained how she'd looked at each singer and asked a question:

"Baby, how long you been off that crack cocaine stuff?"
"Son, how long you been out of jail?"
"Honey, how long you been off the streets whoring around?"

Each answer brought shouts of joy, dancing, and tears of gratitude as the redeemed testified, "I'm free! I'm free! I'm free!" THANK GOD I'M FREE!!!

Then the Bishop thundered, **"If God has set you free from *anything*, you, too, have a reason to Praise the Lord!"** And the Camp Meeting service erupted in celebration and praise!

That message laid the foundation for the song: THE LORD IS WORTHY OF MY PRAISE!

The Song Came Easy

The song was written after Bishop Carpenter told the story at Camp Meeting. And, because I was in attendance, in that very Evangelism meeting in Atlanta, and I witnessed those singers, and that pastor, and that moving of the Spirit that he had described, it allowed me to express in that 3rd verse exactly what he was conveying to that camp meeting crowd.

So do not try to stop me,
My dance, my praise, my joy.
You don't know where He brought me from,
The pain, the guilt, the shame.
He reached way down and saved me,
Washed my sins away.
He set my feet on Higher Ground;
I'll praise His name today!

Thinking about that night in Atlanta, along with Brother Carpenter's account at the Camp meeting, allowed the words to flow. And with that, a song was born, inspired by Bishop Carpenter.

Years later, at the 2019 Falcon Camp Meeting, I stood humbled as hundreds danced in the Spirit and sang the verses of this song around those Camp Meeting altars. It felt like the message, and the man who inspired the song was right there with us in the service again.

THANK GOD FOR MERCY

MERCY365

A PRAYER THAT THERE BE CELEBRATION IN GOD'S HOUSE

Dear Lord,

Today, we thank You for the opportunity to give You praise and honor. You're Worthy Of The Praise!

We thank You that You have personally done a work in our lives, and because of that work, each of us has a testimony and an assignment to share what the Lord has done for us. We must not keep it to ourselves.

We have a reason to shout. We have a reason to praise. We could have been dead. We could have been on the side of the road. We could have been lost without God or His Son. But thank You, Lord, for life, and thank You for the forgiveness of our sins.

Because of Your mercy and grace, there is within us a reason to clap our hands, a reason to stand on our feet, a reason to celebrate the goodness of God.

And Lord, may that celebration never grow silent.

Let our praise be contagious. Let it spread into other lives, other homes, other communities, and other churches.

Send a revival of celebration, joy, and victory among Your people. Remind us that **the joy of the Lord is our strength**, and let that joy rise up in our hearts again and again.

We thank You, and we praise You.

In the Name of Jesus Christ.

Amen.

The Lord Is Worthy of My Praise

Inspired by a Message and Story from Bishop Ronald S. Carpenter Sr.

Written in July 1992

CHORUS

The Lord is great, and worthy of my praise.
Oh yes, the Lord is great, and worthy of my praise.
I said, "The Lord is great, and worthy of my praise."
He woke me up this morning, started me on my way.
(He) gave me food and shelter, told me not to be afraid.
You know, the Lord is worthy of my praise.

VERSE 1

Oh, I'm so glad He saved me, gave me a brand-new song.
He sanctified, baptized, filled me with the Holy Ghost.
That is why I praise Him. That's why I sing and shout.
When I was in sin's prison, the Lord, He brought me out.

CHORUS

The Lord is great, and worthy of my praise.
Oh yes, the Lord is great, and worthy of my praise.
I said, "The Lord is great, and worthy of my praise."
He woke me up this morning, started me on my way.
(He) gave me food and shelter, told me not to be afraid.
You know, the Lord is worthy of my praise.

VERSE 2

I'll praise Him in the morning. I'll praise Him night and noon.
I'll praise Him in the valley. I know my mountain's coming soon.
My hands were made to praise Him,

My feet were made to dance,
I've learned to praise my blessed Lord in any circumstance.

VERSE 3
So do not try to stop me,
My dance, my praise, my joy.
You don't know where He brought me from,
The pain, the guilt, the shame.
He reached way down and saved me,
Washed my sins away.
He set my feet on higher ground; I'll praise His name today!

CHORUS
The Lord is great, and worthy of my praise.
Oh yes, the Lord is great, and worthy of my praise.
I said, "The Lord is great, and worthy of my praise."
He woke me up this morning, started me on my way.
(He) gave me food and shelter, told me not to be afraid.
You know, the Lord is worthy of my praise.

The Lord Is Worthy of Our Praise

Praise ye the Lord. Praise God in His sanctuary: praise Him in the firmament of His power.
Praise Him for His mighty acts: praise Him according to His excellent greatness.
Praise Him with the sound of the trumpet: praise Him with the psaltery and harp.
Praise Him with the timbrel and dance: praise Him with stringed instruments and organs.
Praise Him upon the loud cymbals: praise Him upon the high-sounding cymbals.
Let everything that hath breath praise the Lord. Praise ye the Lord.
Psalm 150 (KJV)

Great is the Lord, and greatly to be praised...
Psalm 145:3 (KJV)

CHAPTER EIGHTEEN

Glory to God in the Highest

And the angel said unto them, Fear not: for, behold, I bring you good tidings of great joy, which shall be to all people. For unto you is born this day in the city of David a Saviour, which is Christ the Lord. And this shall be a sign unto you; Ye shall find the babe wrapped in swaddling clothes, lying in a manger. And suddenly there was with the angel a multitude of the heavenly host praising God, and saying, Glory to God in the highest, and on earth peace, good will toward men.
Luke 2:10-14 (KJV)

I was preparing a Christmas sermon and reading from Luke chapter two, what we call the Christmas Story.

As I sat at my desk, I began rocking back and forth, repeating those words: **"Glory to God in the Highest... Peace on Earth... Goodwill toward men..."**

Over and over, it felt like a song was being birthed. Before I left my desk, the chorus was written.

The next day at church, we sang it repeatedly, and it stirred something powerful within the people — much as it had in me the night before.

Scripture says the angels were saying those words, but in my spirit, I could only imagine them singing — exuberant, joyful, heaven-filled singing.

And why not? God Himself had just stepped into flesh. Emmanuel — God With Us. No wonder the angels rejoiced.
For weeks, we sang the Chorus because that's all I had. So I began asking God to give me a verse. It wasn't long, and verse one was written.

Verse One: Paul and Silas

While reading Acts chapter 16 — Paul and Silas in prison — I wondered: What might they have sung through the midnight hour?

Scripture doesn't tell us. But I imagined they might have sung the same words the angels sang at Christ's birth.

Verse 1:

Paul and Silas, locked in prison,
Didn't know what to do.
They sang and prayed through the midnight hour,
Knew God would see them through.
The ground started shaking, bars started breaking,
Everyone's bands were loosed,
The glory came down, spread over the town,
You could hear the multitude singing...

Then, Verse two:

Verse Two: Elijah on Mount Carmel

Another powerful biblical moment came to my heart — the showdown on Mount Carmel.

Verse 2:
On Mt. Carmel, people prayed
To a god whose name was Baal.
They prayed and prayed and prayed and prayed,
But they prayed to no avail.
Elijah said, "Get ready, folks...
Will the real God please stand up?"
Then the fire fell,
And the prophets of Baal cried,
"The LORD — He is God!"

Months later, God would give another verse, and actually several others.

Verse Three: Testimony of a Friend

I was running from the Lord many years ago,
Liquor bottle in my hand... lost my car, lost my home, everything I owned.
Life was just a great big mess.
Then the preacher preached about the love of God as I had never understood.
To the altar I ran, I began to repent.

And the Lord gave me a new song. It Was…

Glory to God in the Highest,
Peace on Earth, Good Will Toward Men.
Glory to God in the Highest,
Peace on Earth, Good Will Toward Men.
Glory to God in the Highest,
Peace on Earth, Good Will Toward Men.
Peace on Earth…Good Will Toward Men.

A Song Born in Scripture and Experience

The chorus was written almost word-for-word from Scripture. The verses came as I considered the Word of God and reflected on God's faithfulness in both the Old and the New Testaments.

I pray that every Christmas, and every day before and after Christmas, you remember: Where darkness is great, the Light shines even brighter, and where hearts are heavy, Heaven still sings — "Glory to God in the Highest."

I Dedicate This Song to Sister Myrtle Pierce

Myrtle Pierce is one person I think about every time I hear this song. Myrtle was very sick in body, yet that song lived deeply within her. I can still see it as if it were yesterday. Whenever the doctor or nurse walked into her room, she would lift her hand, point toward them, and begin to recite the words of the song. Most times, she didn't just say it; she sang it.

Or, if a family member walked in, she would point toward them and sing with her sweet voice.
"O, Glory to God in the highest, peace on earth, goodwill toward men."

If anybody in this world ever took that song to heart and enjoyed it, Myrtle Pierce did.

And somehow, I imagine the moment I see her in heaven, the very first thing she will do is point towards me, and with that familiar joyful smile declare, "O, Glory to God in the Highest, Peace on Earth, Goodwill toward men."

THANK GOD FOR MERCY

MERCY365

A PRAISE FOR GOD'S GOODNESS

Dear Lord,

With all our hearts, we cry out, **"Glory to God in the highest, peace on earth, goodwill toward men."**

We thank You for being so good to us. Thank You for watching over us day and night. Thank You that Your mercy is renewed every single morning.

With grateful hearts, we say thank You for Your goodness.

In this song of praise and worship, we thank You for being our Lord and our Savior. From the very depths of our being, we lift our voices again and say, **Glory to God in the highest, peace on earth, goodwill toward men.**

With everything within us, we give You thanks. We give You glory for the things You have done, the way You have made, the paths You have paved, and the lives You have changed.

Lord, receive our praise and thanksgiving. You Are Worthy of it All!!!!

In the name of Jesus Christ, we pray.

Amen.

Glory to God in the Highest

written Christmas 2012

CHORUS

Glory to God in the Highest,
Peace on Earth, Good Will Toward Men.
Glory to God in the Highest,
Peace on Earth, Good Will Toward Men.
Glory to God in the Highest,
Peace on Earth, Good Will Toward Men.
Peace on Earth, Good Will Toward Men.

VERSE 1

Paul and Silas, locked in prison,
Didn't know what to do.
They sang and prayed through the midnight hour,
Knew God would see them through.
The ground started shaking, bars started breaking,
Everyone's bands were loosed,
The glory came down, spread over the town,
You could hear the multitude singing…

CHORUS

VERSE 2

On Mt. Carmel, people prayed,
To a god whose name was Baal.
They prayed and prayed and prayed and prayed,
But they prayed to no avail.
Elijah said, "Get ready, folks…

Will the real God please stand up?"
Then the fire fell,
And the prophets of Baal cried, "The LORD — He is God!"

CHORUS
Glory to God in the Highest,
Peace on Earth, Good Will Toward Men.
Glory to God in the Highest,
Peace on Earth, Good Will Toward Men.
Glory to God in the Highest,
Peace on Earth, Good Will Toward Men.
Peace on Earth, Good Will Toward Men.

Part Five

Mercy at Sunset

Most of the songs I have written throughout my life have carried the sound of heaven in them. Many of them speak about eternity, about facing the sunset of our lives with hope.

Over the years, some have called me an escapist because they disagree with my eschatological views concerning the Lord's return for His people. I understand that not everyone sees prophecy the same way, but my longing for heaven has never been about escape. It has always been about expectation as promised by the Lord Himself. He said, "If it were not so, I would have told you" John 14 (KJV).

This section is about the promise of everlasting life. It speaks of the Mercy of God that sustains us when we say goodnight to a loved one… and for when we prepare, one day, to say goodnight for our own celestial departure.

For me, sunset is not the end.
It is the beginning of the everlasting, promised beginning.

Because mercy does not retire.
Mercy does not weaken.
Mercy walks with us all the way from here… to home.

CHAPTER NINETEEN

Home At Last

In my Father's house are many Mansions/Rooms; if it were not so, would I have told you that I am going there to prepare a place for you? And if I go and prepare a place for you, I will come back and take you to be with me that you may also be where I am.
John 14:2-3 (NIV)

Traveling Home

No matter where your travels begin, whether for a vacation, to a friend's or neighbor's house, to a convention, a conference, or to a city in a foreign land. If you're like me, your heart is quietly set on the moment you return home.

When you leave for an extended time, there are things you put in place to give your mind peace while you're gone: the mail is secured, packages are held, the house is watched, and everything is locked and guarded. On long extended trips or short weekend getaways, you will eventually hear someone say, "I sure do look forward to getting back home."

I can say this from experience. I've traveled my share—Israel three times, Honduras twice, Haiti five times, Mexico, the Dominican Republic, and even a World Missions Conference in Canada. I have seen some of the most beautiful places on this earth, places that take your breath away. Yet of all the places I have ever beheld, none compares to a place called HOME.

A Dream of Heaven

In 1995, I was traveling along Highway 70 just outside Kinston, North Carolina. A few nights earlier, I had a dream about Heaven. The beauty of that city was beyond words.

In my dream, I saw a city so fair. No one was crying, not one single tear. My grandmother and friends from the past were there. I knew without a doubt that that was home at last.

It stayed on my heart as I traveled that day. Over and over in my mind, I rehearsed the things John the Revelator said that he saw as read in Revelation 21:

A city of **no more**.

No more death.
No more heartache.
No more pain.
No more suffering.
No more separation.
No more trying to explain the unexplainable.
No more restless nights.
No more tears.
No more fears.
No more binding the enemy.
Just glory. Just peace.
and the presence of God Forever.

HEAVEN!!!

After all that thinking and praying and praising God, I pulled over and began to write down the words God gave me. HOME AT LAST.

This song has been sung countless times, often at homegoing services, reminding everyone of the joy that awaits us in Heaven. Wherever we travel in this life, the best part of the journey is getting home—and one day, we will truly be home at last.

The Saddest Words in the Bible

Probably the saddest words in all of Scripture come from Matthew 25, where Jesus speaks about eternity, sheep and goats, and the separation of humanity before God. He says

"Then shall He say also unto them on the left hand, 'Depart from Me, ye cursed, into everlasting fire, prepared for the devil and his angels.'"
Matthew 25:41 (NKJV)

Over the years, I've preached and exhorted congregations not to allow a goat to steal your joy or rob you of your victory. But there will come a day when God Himself will separate right from wrong, and the sheep from the goats. The goats will spend eternity where goats belong, and the sheep will dwell in the safety, provision, and presence of the Good Shepherd.
To me, nothing compares to the sorrow in those words: the realization that God never intended for any human soul to spend eternity in Hell. Hell was prepared for the devil and his angels, not for you or me. Yet generation after generation, people push

past God's warnings, past His mercy, past His love—and keep pressing forward on their own terms.

This generation seems to have lost the holy fear of Almighty God. Many have redefined right and wrong, calling evil good and good evil. But make no mistake: there will come a day when the sheep are separated from the goats, and truth will be revealed.

The Sword of Separation

Jesus didn't come to make everyone comfortable or to make all things great. He came to divide, to distinguish, to call out what is true and reject what is false. He said, "Think not that I am come to bring peace on earth: I came not to bring peace, but a sword." (Matthew 10:34, NKJV)

The sword is spiritual—it represents a line of distinction. You cannot serve two masters. You will love one and reject the other. You will serve one and despise the other (Matthew 6:24).

Matthew 25 is not only about judgment—it is about the mission of the Church. The Church exists to call people out of darkness and into the marvelous light of Jesus Christ. We are here to help people get ready to meet God.

BTW- Are You Ready For Eternity?

Every person will spend eternity somewhere. The decision is not complex: it boils down to this—are you obeying Christ's commandments, and do you know where you will spend eternity?

There are not three options. There are not five options. There are only two: Heaven or Hell. How you respond to the Holy Spirit's call determines your eternal home.

I'm not saying you must be perfect. But you must be born again, as Jesus teaches in John 3. If you've gotten off track after once giving your heart to God, this is your moment to return.
If you've messed up—fess up.

Then get up and get back in the race.

We live in a world where right is called wrong, wrong is called right, and sin is considered "okay." But sin cannot enter the glorious city called Heaven. I plead with you— if you are heading the wrong way, turn around. God's hand is still open to receive you.

Joshua said, "But as for me and my house, we will serve the Lord."

A Final Plea

If you have never asked Jesus to be the Lord of your life, hear this plea: Eternity is real. You will spend it somewhere. Heaven offers reunion, joy, and peace with God and loved ones. Hell offers separation, suffering, and eternal regret.

Please do not ignore the call. Do not harden your heart. Let God separate you now—not as a goat cast aside, but as one of His sheep, gathered safely in His fold.

Remember the song. Remember the dream. And remember this truth: one day, we will all go HOME AT LAST.

Just exactly where will your home be?

That is the real question.

THANK GOD FOR MERCY

MERCY365

A SUNSET PRAYER

Dear Lord,

We thank You that we can come boldly before Your throne of grace.

Today, we come with the awareness that many people are carrying the heavy burden of grief. Yet we are thankful that we do not weep as those who have no hope.

Please guide us as this song is shared, and let its message speak to hearts and lives in the days to come.

I pray especially for those grieving who have recently lost a loved one. As the words of this song are heard, "*Home at Last,*" may comfort and peace come to every hurting heart.

Home at last. Home at last
The river is clear.
There is not one tear.

Lord, remind us all that one day we will stand before You. Whether we leave this world by a hole in the ground or the hole in the sky, we will one day answer to the King of KINGS. Jesus.

So help us to lay aside childish ways and attitudes, and help us to live our lives in a way that is pleasing to You.

Prepare our hearts for that day, and help us to live with hope, faith, and readiness until we reach our eternal home. Home At Last.

In the Name of Jesus Christ, we pray.

Amen.

"HOME" AT LAST

VERSE 1

I dreamed of a city, a city so fair,
There was no one crying, not one single tear.
There stood my dear grandma and friends from the past.
And I knew without a doubt that I was home at last.

CHORUS

Home at last, home at last.
The river is clear, there's not one tear—home at last.
The crippled are walking, blind eyes see.
Oh, what awaits you and me
When we're home at last,
Home at Last.

VERSE 2

Now don't be discouraged, and don't hang your head.
You see the lights of that grand city are shining just up ahead.
T'will be in a sudden moment, in the twinkling of an eye—
Old things are passed,
As the trumpets blast,
And we will shout, "I'm Home At Last!"

CHORUS

CHAPTER TWENTY

When We Meet Again

Now I saw a new heaven and a new earth, for the first heaven and the first earth had passed away. Also, there was no more sea. [2] Then I, John, saw the holy city, New Jerusalem, coming down out of heaven from God, prepared as a bride adorned for her husband. [3] And I heard a loud voice from heaven saying, "Behold, the tabernacle of God is with men, and He will dwell with them, and they shall be His people. God Himself will be with them and be their God. [4] And God will wipe away every tear from their eyes; there shall be no more death, nor sorrow, nor crying. There shall be no more pain, for the former things have passed away."
Revelation 21 (NKJV)

[51] Behold, I shew you a mystery; We shall not all sleep, but we shall all be changed, [52] In a moment, in the twinkling of an eye, at the last trump: for the trumpet shall sound, and the dead shall be raised incorruptible, and we shall be changed.
1 Corinthians 15 (NKJV)

[2] And He Himself is the propitiation for our sins, and not for ours only but also for the whole world. [3] Now by this we know that we know Him, if we keep His commandments.
1 John 2:2-3 (NKJV)

Mark it down, my friend. Change is coming, and what we lack or are insufficient in spiritually, according to 1 John 2:2, Jesus Christ will make up the difference, if you will sincerely trust in him and allow him to be your Lord and Savior (1 John 2:3).

There are moments in life that only Heaven could have arranged, and the day I met Virginia King (Jenny) was one of them.

It was 1973. I was a seventeen-year-old preacher boy, and she was a fourteen-year-old beautiful girl from the north side of Wilmington.

We met at Cape Fear Memorial Hospital—not exactly the place most people find love, but God had His own plans in motion. Jenny's father, Mr. Robert Earl King Sr., had been injured on the job and was hospitalized. My pastor's daughter, Patricia Wood, was in the next room, also a patient. Somehow, she and Jenny met and struck up a conversation. Pat, as they called her, told Jenny that there was someone she wanted her to meet—and that someone was me.

One day, I stopped by the hospital to have prayer with Pat, and Jenny happened to overhear my prayer from the next room. That day, Jenny and I met for the first time.

Two years later, we began dating. Then, on April 3, 1976, we stood before a packed house at the altar of the Wilmington Freewill Holiness Church with Reverend George Fowler and Reverend Jerold Lewis officiating, and became husband and wife.

April 3, 2026, marks fifty years of marriage, and I can truly say— Jenny has been my faithful partner, my prayer warrior, my best friend, and the love of my life.

Jenny's father, Mr. King, never got over his work accident before our wedding, and he certainly had his share of good days and bad days, but all in all, he was a man full of happiness and humor. He and I enjoyed hobbies together and became great CB buddies. He was *the Port City Seagull,* and I was *the Holy Land Man*, or at least those were our CB call handles. Mr. King treated me more like a son than a son-in-law.

The Room

I'll never forget, on a hot August day in 1996, my family returning home from Dallas, Texas, after attending the IPHC Teen Talent competition with our Church. Our first stop was the hospital where Mr. King had been admitted again. We were hopeful that he would soon recover and come home. But this time, the news was different.

We received the call—"He's not breathing on his own"—so we hurried to the New Hanover Memorial Hospital in Wilmington. Walking down that hallway, I knew where we were headed—"The Room."

As a pastor, I'd stood in that kind of room many times with grieving families, but that day, my family was the one needing comfort.

The doctor came in and delivered the words no one ever wants to hear: "He's passed."

We had just seen him before we went to Dallas, TX. Surely he couldn't be that sick. This was not the news that we were expecting. Our hearts were breaking.

I remember calling my mother to tell her the news, but when I opened my mouth, no words would come out. It wasn't a loud cry—it was a silent, aching cry, the kind that comes from deep within your soul. For nearly three minutes, I couldn't speak. My mother waited patiently on the line until I could finally whisper the words, "Jenny's daddy has passed."

Later that night, still broken but held together by the peace of God, I sat down and wrote the song that flowed straight from my heart: "I Won't Have to Cry When We Meet Again."

That song was my way of honoring a man I dearly loved. It was a song from the heart expressing the hope we have in Christ—that one glad day, there will be no more tears.

Mr. King was so proud that his son-in-law was a preacher. When we'd walk into a restaurant, he'd introduce me with a smile: "This is my son, Reverend Ray Faircloth."

I'd blush and say, "You can leave the Reverend part off, Dad."

But the truth is, I appreciated his respect for the ministry calling upon my life. I called him *Dad,* and I meant it. He wasn't my biological father, but he was a great dad—a man of quiet strength and deep faith in God.

I don't know exactly how introductions happen in Heaven, but I have a feeling that when I enter those gates, I'll see him standing there. And in my heart, I can somehow imagine him saying something like:

"Jesus, this was my son-in-law. He preached Your Gospel and married my daughter Jenny. Jesus, meet Reverend Raymond Faircloth."

And I believe Jesus will smile, and I certainly hope to hear him say. "Well done, good and faithful servant."

THANK GOD FOR MERCY

MERCY365

PRAYER FOR THOSE GRIEVING

Dear Lord,

I believe it is pleasing to You when we lift up our brothers and sisters who are grieving.

We understand that everyone grieves differently. There is no single right way or wrong way to grieve. Each heart carries its own sorrow, and each life carries its own memories and ways to remember.

Lord, there are many among us who have lost someone dear, a spouse, a husband, a wife, a son, or a daughter. And they are learning to walk through the difficult valley of grief.

So today I ask that You would give them wisdom, comfort, and strength for the days ahead. Surround them with Your peace and remind them that You are near to the brokenhearted.

I pray that the Spirit of the Lord would rise up within them. Anoint this prayer with Your presence and let Your power flow through it. Capture the anointing of the moment and release it unto the reader.

May the unity and compassion expressed in this prayer reach beyond these pages, touch hearts, and change lives.

Bring comfort where there is sorrow, hope where there is heaviness, and peace where there is pain.

In the Name of Jesus Christ, we pray.

Amen. Amen.

When We Meet Again

VERSE 1

I've seen the pain you've bore so long,
I've seen your trembling hands.
And oh, the days, the weeks, the months,
We've tried to understand.
But the will of God we lean upon for our God knows it all,
Come morning time, the sun will shine.
Where nobody will grow old.

CHORUS

I won't have to cry when we meet again.
There'll be no more goodbyes,
When we reach Beulah land.
I love you, and I miss you, but by faith one glad day,
We'll stroll the streets of heaven,
Where all pain has passed away.

VERSE 2

Life is like a vapor, a flower in the grass.
It seems before we turn around,
So many years have passed,
But there's a land beyond this veil of tears
Where we'll meet one glorious day,
So wait for me,
What a time it'll be on that coronation day.

CHORUS

CHAPTER TWENTY-ONE

There is a City

But I would not have you to be ignorant, brethren, concerning them which are asleep, that ye sorrow not, even as others which have no hope. I Thessalonians 4 KJV

The Promise of Heaven and Eternal Life

Throughout my life, I've stood by bedsides and gravesides, in living rooms and hospital rooms, watching the people I love make their final journey to a place called Heaven, transitioning from the terrestrial to the celestial.

Like everyone else, I've lost many family members one by one. My dad passed away in May of 1997. My mother passed away in January of 2006. My oldest brother was only 61 when he stepped across the divide in May of 2011. Charlie left us in April of 2013. Willie transitioned to Glory in October of 2024, and Jerry left us in June of 2025. One by one, they left this world behind and went on to the place that I have sung about, preached about, and written about for most of my life.

Jenny has also walked this road. Together, we have buried our mothers and fathers. We have said goodbye to grandparents, uncles and aunts, and the people who shaped our childhoods. We have seen death up close, very close, and we have felt the sting of it. The Bible calls death an enemy, and when you stand there watching the life leave someone you love, you understand why. It wounds, it separates, and it breaks the heart.

And yet, death does not have the final say. It never has had the final say, and it never will. Even though we sorrow, we do not sorrow as those who have no hope. The Scriptures remind us again and again that there is coming a day when this enemy will be destroyed forever. There's coming a day when there will be no more death, no more sorrow, no more sickness, and no more pain. There's coming a day when the last tear will be wiped away, when the last goodbye will be spoken, and when the last grave will be filled. Heaven is not just a dream for the hurting; it is the promised destiny for the redeemed.

Many of the songs I have written through the years have been about that place called Heaven, and about the things that await us on the other side.

Songs like "Don't That Sound Just Like Heaven" tell the story of the deep longing to step into the presence of the One who redeemed us. When my family members left this world, those songs became more than lyrics. They became life rafts for my soul. They ministered to me in the quiet moments when the shock faded, and the grief settled in. They reminded me that death is not the end of the journey, only the beginning.

And I saw a new heaven and a new earth: for the first heaven and the first earth were passed away; and there was no more sea.
[2] And I, John, saw the holy city, new Jerusalem, coming down from God out of heaven, prepared as a bride adorned for her husband.
[3] And I heard a great voice out of heaven saying, Behold, the tabernacle of God is with men, and he will dwell with them, and they shall be his people, and God himself shall be with them, and be their God.
[4] And God shall wipe away all tears from their eyes; and there shall be no more death, neither sorrow, nor crying, neither shall there be any more pain: for the former things are passed away.
Revelation 21:1 (KJV)

John the Revelator looked into that city and saw that there was no more dying, no more heartbreak. I realized that much of what John described is considered hyperbole, his way of trying to give us the best picture he could. But as Paul reminds us, 1 Cor 2:9 "Eye has not seen, nor ear heard, neither has it entered into the heart of man the things that God has prepared for those who love Him."

Even with John's descriptions, the very best we can imagine in our earthly minds about heaven… still falls short. John painted the picture as vividly as he could, yet the reality is far greater, a place of total perfection, a place with absolutely no disappointments, a place where words fail to capture the fullness of joy. Think about it, a place where the enemy can no longer harm or destroy.

There is a city called Heaven, and the builder and maker is God Himself. Living here in this old, corrupt world is only temporary. We are just pilgrims and strangers here.

My dear friend Thomas Brittenham passed away in 2025, leaving behind memories that will never fade. Several years before his passing, Thomas experienced a moment that would forever change the way he and most who knew him thought about heaven.

During that time, Thomas had a serious medical episode at the hospital. There was a moment when it seemed that they had lost him, and everyone feared the worst. But through God's grace, they were able to bring him back. He survived that close call, and the experience stayed with him for the rest of his life.

Afterward, Thomas began to share what he had experienced in his near-death episode. He testified that he had visited heaven. Though words can never fully capture such a place, Thomas did his best to describe it. He spoke of the peace that he felt, the little sheep that he saw, and the little children gathered around Jesus. He marveled at the beauty and the calm that surrounded him, and he often submitted that he didn't understand why he had to come back. The Peace he experienced was beyond his words.

Thomas shared the vision experience with his family and friends. He painted what he could with words, trying to explain the indescribable. We listened and were awed by his testimony, yet we knew none of us could fully grasp the glory of what he saw. John described it beautifully in the book of Revelation, but we are still left trying to understand the fullness of what heaven will be like.

One thing, however, is certain: Thomas is now in that city. He has entered the place he described as best he could, a place more beautiful than anything we can imagine. And though we remain on this side, still trying to picture it and still learning to trust God's promises, we can hold onto the truth that what awaits us is extraordinary, it's a place like no other, a place of eternal peace, love, illuminated by God's Glory.

Heaven is not just a distant dream; it is our eternal home if we trust Jesus to be our Lord and Savior.

The Mystery That Awaits Us

What Heaven will truly be like, none of us fully know. Even John the Revelator, under the inspiration of the Holy Spirit, could only describe it the best he could. Paul said that eyes have not seen, ears have not heard, neither has it entered into the heart of man the things that God has prepared for those who love Him.

So, whatever I have visualized and tried to describe in my songs, whatever I have preached in my sermons, and whatever I have pictured in my mind, I believe Heaven is better, far better, beyond my words, beyond the reach of our imagination.

There will be a reunion there. I plan to see my mother and father again. I'm looking forward to seeing my brothers again. I'm going to see the ones who helped shape my life and ministry. And above all, I will see Jesus, the One who made Heaven possible, the One who offered forgiveness to my wretched soul,

Jesus, the One who conquered death and removed the sting so that we could live forever.

If these songs about heaven have helped me through my valley of the shadow of death, perhaps they will help you through yours. If they have comforted me after saying goodbye, perhaps they will comfort you when the hour comes for you to let go of someone you love. Heaven is not just a theological subject… it is a place I am going, a place I am longing for, and a place where more and more of my family now resides.

Heaven is real. Heaven is promised. And Heaven is closer than we think. Our loved ones are there with the LORD. The LORD is here with us. A Grand Reunion Can't Be Too Far Away.

Heaven

I've mentioned my brother Willie. In the fall of 2024, after years of dialysis and pain, he told his family, "Enough is enough, I'm going to heaven to be with Jesus," and he meant it. **He was ready to live, and he was ready to die.**

His faith was firm, and his peace was settled. In those final days, our family gathered around his bedside. We sang, prayed, laughed, and remembered. And, most of all, we were all overwhelmed by God's Amazing Mercy and Grace that was present in that house.

On Willie's final Thursday morning, he tuned into his 7 a.m. weekly online Men's Bible study. Somewhere in the midst of it, his son Billy let the other men know that they would be signing off so he could take care of his dad. What they didn't know was that Willie was signing off for the last time. Moments later, my brother, William Earl Faircloth, entered eternal peace, to be home with his Lord and Savior, Jesus Christ.

Reminiscing back to a Revival service at the Wrightsville Ave Church of God, where I witnessed Willie surrender his life to Jesus, certainly made this homecoming event bittersweet. Knowing of a surety, that he was absent from us.... But all who knew Willie knew without a doubt that he was now present with the LORD.

God's Promise To the Believer

51 Behold, I shew you a mystery; We shall not all sleep, but we shall all be changed,
52 In a moment, in the twinkling of an eye, at the last trump: for the trumpet shall sound, and the dead shall be raised incorruptible, and we shall be changed.
53 For this corruptible must put on incorruption, and this mortal must put on immortality.
54 So when this corruptible shall have put on incorruption, and this mortal shall have put on immortality, then shall be brought to pass the saying that is written, Death is swallowed up in victory.
55 O death, where is thy sting? O grave, where is thy victory?
56 The sting of death is sin, and the strength of sin is the law.
57 But thanks be to God, which giveth us the victory through our Lord Jesus Christ.
1 Corinthians 15: 51-57 (KJV)

THANK GOD FOR MERCY

MERCY365

A PRAYER OF PRAISE FOR THE PROMISED CITY OF GOD THAT AWAITS US

Dear Lord,

We thank You for the promise of our eternal home. I thank You that this is not heaven, and this is not hell. There is a heaven to gain and a hell to shun. But heaven for the believer is promised, and it lies before us.

As John saw that holy city coming down from God out of heaven, we look forward to that glorious day. How we await the moment when we will gather together again with loved ones who have gone on before us!

There will be no sickness there, no suffering, no sorrow, no crying, no heartache, and no pain.

So right now, Lord, we give You praise and thanksgiving for that glorious city that we await. We are only pilgrims passing through this world, waiting for the city whose builder and maker is God.

And until that glorious morning when we fly away to our heavenly home, we will continue to thank You and praise You.

In Jesus' name,
Amen.

THERE IS A CITY

VERSE 1

There is a city, not made with hands.
There is a city, 'tis a beautiful land.
There is a city that eyes have not seen, ears have not heard,
But it's more than a dream.

CHORUS

"There is a city," John said. "Foursquare."
There is a city. None to compare.
Blind eyes are open. Deaf ears unstopped.
The lame will be walking in the city of God.

VERSE 2

My Daddy is waiting. Grandma is, too.
Loved ones are saying, "Just another hill or two."
Hold on, my brother. It can't be long.
We'll hear the invitation to the city of God.

CHORUS

For there is a city that John said, "Foursquare."
There is a city, none to compare.
Blind eyes are open. Deaf ears unstopped.
The lame will be walking in the city of God.

The Summation of MERCY365

When I began writing this book, it was about my story. My testimony. "This Is My Story. This Is My Song."

The journey God allowed me to walk.

But somewhere along the way, something shifted.
The message became larger than the man.

Mercy grew greater than the experiences I've been through.

It became bigger, broader, more significant than any single chapter of my life. **Those stories can wait until another time.** But the Message of Mercy in my heart must be told. MERCY365.

God has been merciful.

He was merciful in my lifetime. He was merciful to those around me. He was merciful, as I witnessed healing after healing in my life and in the lives of others.

He was merciful in the praise that rose from broken places. He is merciful in the sunset years.

Because of that mercy, I have a reason to praise Him. I have a reason to worship Him.

I have a reason to look toward heaven with hope.
But it all comes back to something deeply personal.

We speak of mercy in our churches. We preach it. We sing about it. We say God wants the prodigal to come home.

But too often, when a prodigal tries to get up from the mud and return, we are the first to doubt them.

"I wonder how long this will last."
"I wonder if it's real this time."
"I wonder when they'll fall again."

Instead of lifting them up, we walk them down the road of suspicion.

I am not looking for loopholes. I'm looking for a Mercy pipeline.

A steady flow.
A continual outpouring.
A church that does not merely quote mercy but becomes mercy.

This final chapter and song are about that truth:

Mercy is more than something we say. It is more than a Scripture we memorize. Mercy is what we do. Mercy is who we are supposed to be.

As God has extended His mercy to us, we must extend agape mercy to others.

Blessed are the merciful, for they shall obtain mercy.
Matthew 5:7 (KJV)

THANK GOD FOR MERCY

MERCY365

CHAPTER TWENTY-TWO

Mercy Is More Than A Scripture

I believe this song is the theme of my latter-day assignment.

The prophet Jeremiah wrote, "It is of the Lord's mercies that we are not consumed, because His compassions fail not. They are new every morning; great is Thy faithfulness." (Lamentations 3:22–23 KJV)

Every new sunrise is proof that God has not given up on us. No matter where we have been or what we have faced, His mercy stands ready to meet us again at the dawn of a brand-new day.

Remember your mercy, O Lord, and your steadfast love, for they have been from of old.
Psalm 25:6 (KJV)

Surely goodness and mercy shall follow me all the days of my life...
Psalm 23:6 (KJV)

For the gifts and calling of God are without repentance.[1]
Romans 11:29 (KJV)

---

1 The phrase "gifts and callings are without repentance" from Romans 11:29 means that God's spiritual gifts and His divine callings His purpose for individuals and nations are irrevocable; He doesn't change His mind, withdraw them, or regret giving them, emphasizing their permanence and God's faithfulness, even if people fall away or don't use them.

The message of Mercy being more than just a Scripture or just something we say as part of our faith is vital to my assignment in closing out this book.

Imperfect folk rely on and absolutely need God's Renewed Mercies every single day. Last time I checked, from the pulpit to the parking lot, we are all Imperfect folk.

Perfect people (or so-called "perfect people") with their religious arsenal of stones will take offense to such a bent towards agape Mercy. This song, "Mercy Is More Than A Scripture," certainly expresses my bent toward forgiveness, redemption, and total restoration for the laity as well as for a Minister. This includes life and ministry after a divorce.

If you've been tripped up or pushed down by the devil, I have a message for you: God's Mercy of Redemption is available, and you can get up and fulfill the calling upon your life.

Though there may be logical exceptions when criminal or legal matters are involved, even at that, after serving as a "Thinking for A Change" and "Moral Reconation Therapy" Facilitator as well as the Senior Chaplain for River's Correctional Facility in Winton, North Carolina, I am a witness to the fact that God can and will redeem the very worst of the worst.

He can restore to a ministry level.... right there in a confined community of corrections. Folks, you can't stop a redeemed man or woman of God from preaching and teaching what they've experienced and witnessed through the life-changing power of the gospel of Jesus Christ.

So, even in a place of confinement, or maybe the prison of your own home… I have a word for you…. **Get Up, My Friend GET UP… IN JESUS' NAME!!**

If this is for you…. Please Get Up!!!

Look upon the fields…. (John 4:35 KJV) They're waiting for you!!! They need you to tell your redemption story!!! Simply tell your story of what God has done for you.

I hope you can sense how passionate I am about God's Mercy and Merciful Restoration. Olan Blackwell, a dear friend in St. Pauls, NC, often said, **"Love is not what you say, Love is what you do."**

We preach about a prodigal who lost his way. And we talk really big and bold about how his father represents our Heavenly Father and is waiting for the son to return home.

According to the scripture, the son comes to his senses, and the father restores him fully, and then some.

But to our very own sons and daughters in this life who trip up and fall, or those who have backslid, we too often make restoration so discouraging, with our religiously complicated hoops higher and more complicated than our cathedral ceilings.

And for some…we shut the door with absolutely no way back home.

Let me say this again: I'm not looking for a loophole of compromise, but I believe there's a **Mercy Pipeline** for the wounded, the fallen, and especially those who feel so rejected.

If God is willing to forgive it, forget it, and cast it into the sea of forgetfulness, then who are we to throw out a net into the sea and try to drag it back up again?

The Call to Rise Again

With every breath in my body, I will proclaim to the fallen: Get **up.**

Rejoice not against me, O mine enemy: when I fall, I shall arise; when I sit in darkness, the LORD shall be a light unto me.
Micah 7:8 (KJV)

Get up and find your place in the will of God. Get up and do what God has called you to do. The devil may have knocked you down, but he cannot keep you down.

And if you've gotten up, let me say, I'm proud of you.

If you're still struggling to rise, I'm here to encourage you: that there's some cool, clear water…. just up ahead.

Get up, my friend.

God called you before your grandmother met your grandfather. His calling on your life did not change because you messed up. The calling and gifts of God are without repentance. He does not change His mind. So, rise, brush off the dust, and take your place.

Mercy still flows, Grace still redeems, and God still Revives and Restores.

MERCY IS MORE THAN
A SERMON ELOQUENTLY SPOKEN!
IT'S MORE THAN WHAT WE SAY!

IT'S FORGIVENESS. IT'S COMPASSION.
MERCY IS WHAT GOD DOES FOR US
AND WHAT GOD'S PEOPLE DO FOR OTHERS!!

THANK GOD FOR MERCY

MERCY365

PRAYER FOR MERCY 24/7, 365

Dear Lord,

As I come to the close of this book, I recognize that the heartbeat of everything written in these pages is found in this final moment.

The reason we do what we do. The reason we preach what we preach. The reason we sing what we sing.

It all comes back to MERCY. And if Mercy is not Mercy365, then it's not Mercy at all.

I believe Mercy is more than something we say. It's more than belonging to a church or carrying a religious title.

Mercy is forgiveness. 365
Mercy is compassion. 365
Mercy is choosing grace when judgment might seem easier.

So Lord, help us to live lives that operate in mercy. Mercy365

Help us to bend on the side of mercy. Mercy365 No matter what others may say or do, help us to take the high road and walk in mercy, love, and grace. (24/7-365)

Let mercy guide our hearts, shape our words, and direct our actions. (24/7-365)

And may the message of mercy continue to live on in every life that reads these pages. MERCY365……..

In Jesus' name we pray.

Amen.

Mercy Is More Than A Scripture

The Gifts and Calling of God on a Nation or an Individual are Irrevocable.

CHORUS

Mercy is more than a scripture.
It's more than something you say.
Mercy is more than a scripture.
It's more than a prayer that we pray.
It's compassion, forgiveness,
It's something God's people do.
Mercy's extended, dear neighbor.
God's Mercy extended to you.

VERSE

So many have stumbled and fallen.
So many have lost their way.
They've tripped and lost balance.
Some fall flat on their face.
But God has called us to action,
By more than mere words that we say.
Go rescue the wounded, the broken;
Show mercy to someone today.

CHORUS

Mercy is more than a scripture.
It's more than something you say.
Mercy is more than a scripture.
It's more than a prayer that we pray.
It's compassion, forgiveness,

It's something God's people do.
Mercy's extended, dear neighbor.
God's Mercy extended to you.

Mercy's extended, dear neighbor.
God's mercies extended to… you.

CONCLUSION

Every life has a beginning, a journey, and a destination. Mine began on Bordeaux Avenue in Wilmington, North Carolina, and in time, it led me to a place called MERCY in Ahoskie, North Carolina. Some would say there was nothing remarkable or extraordinary about such a journey. But for me, the road between those two places has been filled with moments that I can only describe as incredible.

As I've reflected across the years, I am amazed that a young boy from Bordeaux Avenue could one day pastor people who trusted him to preach and pray, and to sing and lead them through the joys and storms of life. The congregations that I've pastored remain humbling testimonies that God's calling does not always fall upon the qualified. But God will qualify the Called.

From Bordeaux Avenue to MERCY Church in Ahoskie, North Carolina, from my Childhood to a Ministry Calling, and from Simple beginnings to Sacred places, this is my testimony of a life shaped by Great Grace and Mercy.

THANK GOD FOR MERCY....

MERCY365

ABOUT THE AUTHOR

Raymond Franklin Faircloth, Sr. was born on April 3, 1956, in Wilmington, North Carolina. He was raised in the Sunset Park community and attended Sunset Park Elementary and Junior High Schools before transferring to John T. Hoggard High School, where he graduated in 1974.

On his birthday, April 3, 1976, Raymond married the love of his life, Virginia Ann King (Jenny). The following year, on August 4, 1977, God blessed them with their first child, Ray Jr., and again on May 31, 1980, with a beautiful baby girl, Melissa Ann.

Though he did not attend a formal seminary or Bible school in his early years, Raymond remained faithful to God's call, serving in pastoral leadership as a Minister of Music, Associate Pastor, and Senior Pastor beginning at the age of twenty.

In later years, he pursued further education to strengthen his ministry skills through the University of Cincinnati, becoming a certified (MRT) Moral Reconation Therapy Facilitator as well as a (T4C) Thinking 4 A Change and (CBISA) Cognitive Behavioral for Substance Abuse Facilitator.

Also, earning a Master of Ministry degree from Southwestern Christian University in Bethany, Oklahoma, and a Doctor of

Ministry (D.Min.) degree from Newburgh Theological Seminary in Newburgh, Indiana.

God called Raymond to preach at just twelve years old. That calling was confirmed when, at the age of fifteen, he was awakened in the night by the stirring of the Holy Spirit. Rising in the early morning hours, he told his parents, Clyde and Minnie Faircloth, that God had called him to preach—and he declared that he would share God's Word even if it meant preaching on a street corner. From that day to this, he has remained steadfast and true to that divine calling.

THANK GOD FOR MERCY

MERCY365

www.ingramcontent.com/pod-product-compliance
Lightning Source LLC
LaVergne TN
LVHW050614100826
845148LV00011B/1578

* 9 7 9 8 8 9 5 9 0 7 5 6 6 *